Signposts
of the
Spiritual
Journey

A Practical Road Map
to a Meaningful Life

WATKINS
Sharing Wisdom Since 1893

Signposts of the Spiritual Journey
John Siddique

First published in the UK and USA in 2021 by
Watkins, an imprint of Watkins Media Limited
Unit 11, Shepperton House, 83–93 Shepperton Road
London N1 3DF

enquiries@watkinspublishing.com

A CIP record for this book is available from the British Library

ISBN: 978-1-78678-517-6 (Paperback)
ISBN: 978-1-78678-611-1 (eBook)

10 9 8 7 6 5 4 3 2 1

Printed in the United Kingdom by TJ Books Ltd.

Typeset by Lapiz

www.watkinspublishing.com

MIX
Paper from
responsible sources
FSC
www.fsc.org   FSC® C013056

For my beautiful son Adonis

CONTENTS

Acknowledgements   1
Introduction   3

PART ONE: TURNING TOWARD LIFE   11

  1 The arising of questions   13
  2 The urge to honestly meet yourself   29
  3 The inner decision to step forward   59
  4 Moving from reaction to response   91

PART TWO: HOMEWARD   109

  5 A clearer sense of choice   111
  6 Moving from fear to love   145
  7 The answer in the question   159
  8 Returning to innocence   167

PART THREE: RIGHT WHERE YOU ARE   179

  9 A deeper normality   181
10 Grace   193
11 Freedom means letting go of letting go   199
12 (You have always been) awakening to a new day   205
13 Losing it   223
14 Not two but not one either   227
15 Always becoming   233
16 Giving everything to love   245

Recommended reading   247
Biography of John Siddique   249

ACKNOWLEDGEMENTS

My deepest gratitude to Alex Joicey, who invited me to write a short essay that directly led to this book coming into existence. I wish to extend my thanks to Fiona Robertson and Daniel Culver, my very kind editors at Watkins, and Steve Marshall, our copyeditor.

Though I am not aligned with any formal religion or tradition, I bow in love and gratitude to those who have walked before and beside me as guides through their teachings, presence and inspiration: Stephen Levine, Donald Shimoda, Paul Brunton, Ramana Maharshi, Sri Nisargadatta, Pema Chodron, Ram Dass, Swami Janakananda, and most especially beloved Sri Swami Satchidananda and my students, who perhaps are my real teachers.

I hold in heart and memory my mum Norah O'Neill and my brother/friend Chris Robinson, both of who left their forms between the previous book and this one.

And of course, all love to my son to whom this book is dedicated, and my wife Abha, who is the reason I am here.

INTRODUCTION

Whatever has led you to pick up this book, please know that you are most welcome here. This book is for anyone who feels the pull to understand more about allowing a greater sense of meaning into their life and the journey that is often called the spiritual path. This welcome extends to you regardless of your background, politics, education, place of birth, or current situation. Because what we are talking about in this little book is realizing the genuine awareness of the truth of who we are before all of those things. This book at heart reflects on the profound evolution that is both natural and inherent to humanity and, therefore, you. Though when we look at the world through the lens of the day's circumstances, things may seem far from progressing consciously.

It's easy to believe that you have to be a certain kind of person to realize sacredness or find the spiritual in your life. Perhaps you have an idea of some kind as to what qualities you think that person may have or that you may not have. But whether you are what the current society calls a good person or not, you are not closed out from life's real purpose. Even if you are someone who has committed the worst of crimes, you are not removed in any way from the truth of what is. We may, for whatever reason, think that we are flawed or irredeemable in some way or that this journey is impossible for a person like us. "If only you knew me, you'd see", you might want to say. I hear this one every day. Not one person who has ever lived or will ever live is removed from the sacred by even a hair's breadth. We might be wholly unconscious of this, and like most people, be living through the things we identify with, but not one of us is lost from sight. The soul is unstainable and is not involved in any of that, no matter how entrenched or large things might look. We may, however, have some work to do to clear our sight so that we may see, and more importantly, realize who we are at the deepest level.

People come to the spiritual path through many routes, from taking up a mindfulness or yoga practice and wanting to know what comes next or from a time of personal crisis in their selfhood or relationships. Often endings or close calls are what begins to open the door for a lot of people. Sometimes it can be the voice of your soul crying out or breaking through the current situation, and for some – there is a sense of something deeper within them, like a constant companion in their lives, or it may be even a combination of these feelings. As you have picked this book up, there must be something calling to you, asking you to step further onto your path, to undertake the most essential journey there is. I invite you to connect with that sense now as these words speak to you.

There are many easily recognizable signposts that can help you see where you are and where you are going. These indicators or signifiers can even point to what is going on in areas that you might not be conscious of yet. It is essential to state here at the outset that the path of awakening, or enlightenment, is not one of asking you to believe in something, but rather, perhaps, reassuring you that it is a path of adventure, of allowing, and ultimately finding out for yourself. You know the reality of the ground under your feet by the sense of authenticity that comes naturally with anything true. Just so, you are invited to lean into that grounded knowing within yourself here too.

As you can see from what we call the news each day, as a species and as tribes and individuals, we tend to cling to conditioned identities that reinforce who we believe we are as people, and as countries and so on. You might recognize that this prevents a great deal of our evolution and potential from taking place both materially and spiritually. However, even these limitations cannot stop life from knocking at your door. Life doesn't ever give up on you. Every moment of every day asks you to be at home in the reality of what is. This is perhaps one of the greatest miracles that shows that the truth is within reach of anyone. It is in reach of you at this very second.

Every moment is the most significant opportunity for meaning and awakening. The taking of the tiniest step, even a trillionth of a millimetre into awareness and away from resistance, is a step that will lead you toward home. Life's essential movement is to lead you to your wholeness and truth. If we look at ourselves and the world without judgement, we will see that we too often resist the motion of life's purpose in almost everything we do.

PAUSE FOR REFLECTION

What did that earlier invitation to connect to what made you pick up this book tell you? Where in you do you feel this urge to step onward?

Ordinariness as the path

The journey of enlightenment is really about your ordinary life. Yes, the one you are living right now. There is no requirement to be someone other than the person you are. The truth is that it is not some distant goal or belief system out there that you have to align yourself with. It is about you and the journey toward congruence and awareness with your soul. In reality, there is no journey to be made, but because we are caught up in things to the level that we are, it can look like a journey, or a job of work, for the longest time. Eventually, you will realize the truth rather than believing in stories of it, and you will see that you have always been whole. That you have never not been your soul. You could not be here and alive in this moment if this were not true. There is no reconnection to be made or belief to believe in. You are not even the space of a single breath away from reality.

This book ...

This book aims to be a friend that walks beside you on your journey. It also hopes to be a map that you can rely on as you find your way to meaning and freedom. This map will not be for everyone and is not an attempt to appeal to as many people as possible. It is for you since you are the one here right now. It has been built simply and honestly by asking the most fundamental questions of who we are. In my own life, I have had one question singing through my existence for as long as I can recall – how do I truly live from my soul? I've been blessed to never have lost sight of this over the decades of my life. This question was essentially the core aspect of my seeking and practice until grace came to show me that living my ordinary human life guided from that deeper place within is the only answer that is required. It is just a matter of awareness and presence, rather than believing and striving. So when you read the word freedom in this book, I mean this awakening for yourself to the truth of what simply is and who you are. In other words, the movement from being separated from life by conditioning and beliefs to awareness of being part of the sacred wholeness of reality.

... and how you might use it

There are four interweaving strands within this book. We will look at the various signposts on the road of enlightenment, and we also will look at the significant blockages that stand in our way at each stage of the journey. We will learn how awareness is the key to everything we are talking about here, and we will turn our inner gaze toward the great vehicle of meditation and its truest purpose, which is to take us along the pathless path to our freedom until such a point that we are ready to receive the truth through grace.

It is important to remind you that you do not have to do any of this. There is no rule to say you must undertake this journey or change in any way. This is because unless you are entirely free to not join in, how can you take part? How can you bring your energy, love and honesty to things? If any of this was a voice saying that you must do this and that, it would be like a nation that describes itself as a democracy but has made it illegal to not stand for their flag or national anthem. Unless we are free not to, we do not have democracy, no matter what the flags and the leaders say. However, if the freedom to choose for yourself without pressure is implicit, then, of course, we may be inclined to stand because we feel valued and respected for our existence. Your life is your life. Your journey is your journey, and your realization is also yours. No one can share their realization with you, but through a book such as this, I can try to light the road for you as best I can. How and when you meet your path is completely up to you.

You might simply read this book because you like spiritual books. Some will read it to prove to themselves that they know better than this guy. Others may simply just be looking for information or be taking a comparative religion or academic approach and so on. All that is fine. But like, say, books on growing potatoes, you can read every book on potatoes and their cultivation and history. You might even be the most highly qualified potato historian in the world, and yet you can do all that and have never tasted a potato. It is my wish for you that you cook those vegetables and make yourself a good nourishing dinner. You can simply read this book through, and then later you might find it calls you back when you are working through something, or you might take your time with it and meet it as a map and a friend as you go through life.

Each chapter describes a particular signpost on the journey that myself and others have witnessed over converging lines of living, observing, reflecting and realizing across thousands of years. The fact that there are 16 signposts is quite arbitrary. Written in another year, there might have been 21 or 90. It's just how it has come out. As you move from signpost to signpost, we will explore the aspects of meaning and awakening in real human terms of what is going on. We will look at the blockages that prevent realization and the things that might arise once you start moving beyond that stage. We will talk very clearly and honestly about things. There is no spiritual bypassing or ego feeding in this book. So keeping kindness, forgiveness, love and a sense of humour about these most serious aspects of life will help us. Each chapter will also offer practices and reflections on what you can do to move on in your journey at each stage.

The book is divided into three parts:

- Part One is about settling into having found yourself on this path.
- Part Two is about when the impetus of your journey moves from that initial start to having a more grounded sense of travelling home within it.
- Part Three is about the arrival home and how things continue from there.

A personal note on the language here

There are words like soul and God throughout this book because those are the words I like to use. I also have used Sanskrit words and words from other languages from time to time when there are no equivalents in English. It is beautiful to acknowledge the lineages and people across the centuries who have contributed to revealing the way to us. I know that many will not allow themselves this book and its author because of things like this. We live in a time when some people won't have even made it past my surname or face to meet what we're sharing here because of their conditioning. They are on their journeys whether they know it or not, and so it is not important at this level. What is most important is your journey home.

We live in a seemingly impossible time where everything
is meant to serve our identities and ideas of who we are.
Those identities are bent to serve the tribalism, duality,
national identities, political interests and the educational
systems of the day. If we don't join in, we are told we are no
one, or even worse. These are aspects of the first and greatest
blockage to our journey and awakening. Heartbreakingly, we
are so often full of who we think we are that we miss out on
ourselves, each other, and things that truly benefit us.

Recognizing this fact, we can choose to meet those who
live life through the lenses we are discussing and say, "May
peace go with you". This work is never about trying to chase
after someone to convince them of anything. The soul does
not care for even one moment about the conditional aspects
that we live through, but we can learn to understand their
existence and how we might use them in a more meaningful
and awareness-based way, and we will talk about this toward
the end of the book.

But here we are

This book is not about trying to encourage you to add another
layer to yourself to sell you the idea that only this way, or
"my way", will complete you and give you some ultimate
experience. It is important to tell you that at no point do
I go along with what is often presented as the spiritual path
– the misconstrued teaching which says that once you realize
presence or awaken, all your human troubles simply go away.
The teacher is the life in you. It is your very own soul. Your
curriculum, if we can call it that, is the very life you have
right now. I hope that this book can walk beside you like a
quiet, experienced friend so that when you have a question
on your journey, you might feel encouraged and supported to
recognize the terrain before you go on your unfolding path of
meaning and self-realization.

PART ONE
TURNING TOWARD LIFE

THE ARISING OF QUESTIONS

Are you looking for me? I am sitting right next to you.
My shoulder is against yours.

*You will not find me in meditation halls, nor in the **mandir**,*
*the **masjid**, the **beyt knesset**, or in the cathedral:*
not in the words of a mass, nor in mantras, or sutras,
not in complicated yoga postures, nor in eating nothing
other than rice and vegetables.

When you sincerely look for me, you will see me instantly –
you will find me with you in the smallest house of time.

Tell me, what is God?

God is the breath inside the breath.
                    (Kabir, 1398–1448 – version by John Siddique)

Regardless of what brings you to the path, the first signpost
is always marked by the arising of questions. Of course, you
will read or hear about a rare few people who spontaneously
awaken. But we can't guarantee that outcome or wish ourselves
into being one of them; only grace brings awakening in the
long or short run, everything else is your journey.

    You are you, and where you are at this moment is where
you are. The here and now is the key to everything. When
awakening takes place it will always be spontaneously through

grace, and never because we've struggled for or wished or intentioned such a thing. Yet like a gardener learning to plant a garden, we may prepare our earth by feeding the soil, understanding the cycles of the sun, the moon, the rain and the earth, creating the best conditions for the seed to open, to flower and fruit. We also discover along the way that a cherry tree cannot become an apple tree, and vice versa, no matter how much we might wish it. As we move into greater awareness, we discover the great miracle of the garden of our own ordinary life.

At this point, you might find yourself questioning what is going on in the world around you, or you may be questioning the purpose of your own life. Anyone who dares to reflect on life and its meaning finds that things tend to boil down to three primary questions. I'll just place the three questions here without commentary because you know them already and, in essence, they are why you are here. You have always known these questions.

- Who am I?
- What am I here for?
- Is there a way to end suffering?

Seven other secondary questions feature prominently throughout the journey, which you will similarly find you already know:

Who? What? Why, Where? When? What if? How?

PAUSE FOR REFLECTION

I invite you to pause for a minute and reread the ten questions above slowly to yourself and see where you feel them in your body, or your energy, concerning your life's journey. You may want to introduce these questions into your journaling from time to time.

Learning to turn toward awareness

You can notice or even encourage a shift within yourself toward awareness by the way you frame your questions as you meet daily life situations. For example, if we allow a movement from asking questions such as "Why is this person doing this to me?" or "Why is (insert personal difficult situation) always happening to me?" and instead try to drop taking the situation personally, and allow appreciation of any other person involved, then we're not coming from the place of it being a problem. Then we can ask things such as:

- How can I bring awareness to what is going on?
- What if I choose to respond rather than react?
- What really would improve the world?
- How do I step out of my way to transcend this situation?
- What if I choose love and forgiveness with this other person?

Notice how these more reflective questions lead to greater awareness if we drop our resistance and allow the momentary vulnerability that comes with this turning around. All of our ten initial questions, if asked with this openness, will take you toward a better way of meeting and experiencing your own life, and other people. We restore our humanity instantly and easily with a simple shift.

As you begin to work more consciously like this, you will start to find that each question contains its own answer. With all of this work, I would encourage you not to search too hard for answers in your mind. Thinking is wonderful and has its place, but we can often go much further by dropping into our hearts and letting the question just exist within ourselves. This way too we begin to be able to stay more open and curious about life. The mind will always come up with its usual commentaries of course – "Yes", "No", "How stupid this is", and so on. Yet as your awareness deepens, you will see that the mind in this mode is only doing its job of trying to protect you by digging into what it already knows as it searches for what to do. The mind without heart and awareness only knows what it has been conditioned with from the process of socialization. This often keeps us limited in our ability to respond and closed to much of life, while unknowing of our real depths and basic goodness.

Our training usually tells us that someone else is responsible for everything that happens to us, and we may be reactive to even the slightest hint of allowing vulnerability. It can seem that our happiness, our love life, our situations, our health, our spirituality and so on, are either the luck of the draw or they are something we have to work very hard at to achieve. Our socialization training also tells us that we need to become a "somebody" who does things in a certain way to have a place in the world, to be loved, to be fed, to belong and to be of value as a human being. Because of what passes for normality through this way that we've been doing things for so long, it is really important to have a good understanding of the process of conditioning, so we will take a good look at how this works over the next couple of chapters.

We tend to believe that these outward motions of thought energy are our lives. This belief makes it seem like the answers we seek can only be found if we are smart enough, or have the right "life situation" or set of experiences in place. At a certain level, of course, all this activity and achievement feels great if it is not crushing us under its wheels. Yet no matter the situation, the voice of the soul is in there asking you: Who am I? What am I here for? As your deeper side starts to communicate more clearly, you might find that you feel that whatever you do is not enough to actually complete you or fulfil you fully. Please know this feeling is a good thing as it is the desire for wholeness. So all we want to do here is move beyond just feeling that and into a gentle place of unfolding that brings us into knowing our soul. Each of us can know and experience our soul, and let our lives be shaped by it. This is the meaningful life we are talking about. This is the journey of awakening or enlightened living.

Before we know this and accept and appreciate the daily steps of our journey, we try pushing deeper into clinging to the conditional objects that we meld our identities with. We push with intensity into our emotional sphere. "I just need more" we say, or we just keep trying to switch things out to find a fit that will make us whole. "Perhaps this isn't the right house, or car, or relationship." We might lean into the pain of our past: "It's what happened in my family when I was young." Or: "if only we got rid of all of this kind of person the world would be alright." Notice how these motions of thought into this type of feeling always seek separation or duality. Then it presents one side of the duality as the answer.

PAUSE FOR REFLECTION

I invite you to kindly take a few minutes to reflect on your self-talk toward yourself and others. Let's not look for guilt or shame, but we're doing this just to see what is there, even if that is blanking out when you try to bring your attention to this place. The first step toward meaningful change is always acknowledgement of the problem. We meet it as best as we can at this particular time.

The second step is to say "hello" to it rather than "go away", and this genuinely will change everything. Perhaps try this with what is arising in you right now. Can you just say hello with your kindness and love and let it be there? What happens next?

The journey begins

It is said that the longest journey in human life is the journey from the head to the heart. It is of paramount importance that we meet our lives, these questions, and what comes from them at the level of the heart. Our minds are the most wonderful tools, but as we shall see further in Signpost 2, the content and systems of the mind are placed within us by both conscious and unconscious conditioning. The ordinary mind has a tendency to be reactive from its unconsciousness, which pushes and pulls us trying to get us to our satisfaction or safety. We do need, at some small level, to satisfy our heads, but enlightenment or awakening is not something you can think your way to – if that were so, the world would look very different than it does right now. The heart at the emotional level can be just as conditioned as the mind; we will look at this too in the next chapter. The ordinary heart at least has the possibility of emotional engagement, and the heart is rightly seen by so many of the spiritualities of the world as being one of the great doorways to truth and the deepest awareness within us that we might call the soul. As Chuang Tzu said:

Don't listen with your ears, listen with your mind.
No, don't listen with your mind, but listen with your spirit.
Listening stops with the ears, the mind stops with
recognition, but spirit is empty and waits on all things.

A SMALL HEART AWARENESS PRACTICE

I invite you to sit upright and simply be aware of the space of the room around you; please don't try to go into or have a meditational experience. Rather, just allow yourself as best you can to be here, and to feel the space of the room around you.

Allow yourself to feel the energy in your body while feeling the space in the room so that you have a physical sense of the life in your body.

As you become more aware of the space in the room and the energy of your body, you might notice that perhaps you feel it more in one hand or one leg, perhaps as vibration, or heat, or sensation. It's all okay.

Allow yourself to be easy for these few moments, don't concentrate or over focus, just use feeling and felt sense as best you can.

You can close your eyes if you like.

(Oh, now you can't read the page.)

Just take a moment like this.

I invite you now to simply place one hand on your heart and take another moment while allowing yourself to simply notice how this feels for you. I will not place any leading words here to suggest to you what you are supposed to feel. This is your journey, please notice for yourself with kindness.

The only reason we are doing this practice is to begin to get to know ourselves in this way.

Is there anything arising or sticky within you at this moment? Can you just say hello to it and let it be there without getting caught in trying to push it away? We are not trying to get rid of anything, but if we meet it like this with kindness we begin the process of reintegration.

Please just let go of all effort now and rest into the space in yourself and the room – the feeling of life in your body.

When you have sat a few moments, you can conclude your practice when you are ready to. Sit like this as long as you feel you want to.

You may wish to journal for a few moments about your experience.

You can use this practice as often as you like; it will be different every time you do it.

The first great blockage

One day, Jesus invited a little child to stand among his group. "Truly I tell you," he said, "unless you change and become like little children, you will never enter the kingdom of heaven. Therefore, whoever humbles himself like this little child is the greatest in the kingdom of heaven."

The Buddha said: "Your work is to discover your work, and then with all your heart to give yourself to it."

Undoubtedly the greatest blockage to our realization and wholeness is not knowing that the path even exists in the first place. Intellectually we may know, we may come from various faiths and religions and feel like we are on the path. I have even met people who have doctorates in Buddhism, or various aspects of spirituality or mindfulness, yet still find this blockage is there. This is because we often treat things as if they were a subject that can be learned, or information that can be accumulated and debated about. Sometimes we have a faith that needs to be followed or held on to, no matter what presents itself to us. Thankfully we don't need to suddenly try to stop and change, or breakthrough to a different place. This is where hope lies and real steps on the path can be made. You see the only thing that ever works is the smallest shift in awareness; this is the only thing that reveals the greater reality.

All things other than *our* path are not *the* path

Your path is very easy to recognize because it always leads to the heart. This is the reason we have begun with, and will remain with, the heart throughout this teaching. The heart is the organ of response, while we might say that the mind without the heart is the organ of reactivity and continuance. The heart when it is met with awareness is what brings your feet to your path. The wonderful mind for all its abilities cannot do this, though amusingly it often tries to give the impression that it can. If you will reflect a moment, you will see that we cannot think our way to love or freedom, but the heart knows their flavour and so it is our best guide.

Not knowing that there is a way to freedom is the greatest difficulty in the world. We can easily see this ignorance of the truth reflected in every aspect of the world around us, through news, politics, wars, educational systems, patriarchal, authoritarian and separatist ideas, how we use money in the world, as well as the countless personal and global inequities. We take all these things and more to be just the way things are, that these systems cannot be undone and that they are just how it has always been. Within it all, we quite understandably struggle to find happiness and meaning by carving out bubbles of safety and sanctuary in whatever ways we can. We wall all of that out with our materials and our energy, while jailing ourselves into our sense of separateness.

We often hear that the state of the world proves there is no God, but what we are seeing is what our true religions are: duality, separateness, narcissism, righteousness, greed and clinging to delusion. We believe in these things so totally despite what we say or broadcast. If it were not so, the way things are could not be so. This is why the shift to the heart of our awareness is so deeply necessary, and that everything other than this honest step only keeps the duality turning.

Sadly, even what we call science often falls prey to being used as a religion under the models of duality and conditioning – it also has too often gone where the money is or has been used to support particular views, to reinforce political power or business models and so on. I know it will be hard for some of you to read this. So please believe me that I am extraordinarily pro-science. Pure science and spirituality need to have the same goal, to answer the questions of who we are, and why we are here, and how we can be here in a better way. Too often we have thrown too much away in our pretence of rigour and science only to find later that our approach is based on cultural appropriation, supremacist values and continuing dualities. We look for life on Mars but don't care for our neighbour. Will we be any different when we get to Mars, by magic or technology perhaps? Let's keep the best that science offers us and realize that we can pair it with ancient teachings that have come down to us today that are as rigorous as any modern scientific method: true yoga and meditation, the teachings of the rishis, Taoism and *neigong*, Ayurveda, and so on. These should be treated equally in our considerations as they are far older and wiser than we have been brought to believe, and perhaps by removing this separation between science and sacredness we can walk more honourably toward the truth that is the truth.

The way through

There is no need on our journey to try and break through anything. Simple realization, is all that is needed to lead us to transcend our ignorance. This is not a path of ascendance, awakening takes place in the here and now – it is not a question of degrees or achievements. The asking of heart questions, allowing ourselves to notice how things don't quite line up as we are told, and staying open will all switch the light on. This is all that it takes. If you are in a dark room tripping and falling, unable to see what is going on, no amount of flailing, believing, fighting, making intentions, or screaming is going to dispel the darkness. Switch the light on, however, and the room is lit. The switch is the heart, and the light is awareness. Once the light is on, we may find that the room of our life is filled with so many things that are perhaps broken and dirty and uncared for. There will be many beautiful things just sitting there untouched. Once the light shines by even the smallest amount, we can start to clean and make our room a better place to live. That is the invitation of your soul. That you allow yourself to simply switch the light on, or to open the curtains, clean the dirt from the windows. Not to keep on flailing in the dark, or to keep defending the right to stay in the dark broken room, though of course, you do have that right. Your soul wants your beautiful wholeness to live through. This is all a big oversimplified metaphor, I know, but you know what I mean. This is my wish for you as we go onward.

Broadcasting

Reality and truth do not require us to broadcast anything
about who we are or what we know, as it begins to register
within our being. It does not need us to dress a certain way, or
shave our heads, or take a spiritual name, or use a certain way
of speaking. We start by finding the spaces in our reactivity,
within the beliefs we cling to, and all the things that cause us
to live our lives in duality. Our heart-space questions are the
best and kindest way to begin to find the light. Bringing your
heart to the matter is what will engage you in your process and
will help you to bring your basic goodness to your table, and
therefore the table of all beings.

Finding the space within things is the key, and thankfully
every moment and situation in your life will provide a doorway
when met in the way we are discussing. There are so many
openings that you perhaps already sense the love, relief and
possibility of greater depth available to us within the areas of
family life, relationship, friendship, kindness, art, yoga, sport,
love, sexuality, poetry, nature and so on. These are great first
places to allow more heart-space that leads to awareness, then
as we realize our awareness more and more, we will begin to
see that every area of life has this living sacred space within it.

Four tools to help your journey

With the help of the following, we can better begin to see the
wholeness of ourselves, each other and what is:

1. Responsibility and honesty

It can easily look as if we live many lives: work life, family life,
time alone, sexual life, personal life, spiritual life and so on.
We may even think we have to get past some of these to get
to a special time and place when we can just be ourselves. But
you need to realize that every minute of your life is your life:
home, work, family, sex, spiritual, good days and bad days,
healthy days and days of illness. Even if you are dying of the

23

worst cancer, you still know that any moment you are alive in your body is life, and therefore the greatest opportunity you have for awareness and love. The taking of responsibility for the unity and congruence of our lives is the difference between a life of value and a life spent wishing, hoping and forcing - often in futility or desperation.

The application of radical honesty geared toward love while we claim the potency of our own lives is the great compass that will guide our journey. So now you have your vehicle and your guidance system in place.

2. Meditation and prayer

We will talk a lot more about meditation and prayer later on, but for now, I just want to initially flag them up for you to consider. Meditation is what will help you find the space within all the seemingly impossible dense layers and structures that appear to stand in your way. It is also the place where you take time to access the great nourishment of your life and soul.

Prayer is the greatest way we have to offer both our knowing and unknowing into the great space in which we are loved and accepted regardless of what we may or may not have done before this moment.

3. Being teachable

I'm sure you have met many people who are incapable of saying that they "don't know", or who are so full of their knowledge that when you meet them you are simply not met. You might even be that person. I certainly was like this for a great deal of my life. If we are so full like this, we cannot learn anything, cannot meet anyone really, cannot even love another person much outside of objectification. We will debate or argue everything, be reactive rather than able to respond or be kind, and we will always be defending ourselves and our position from a place of fear while falsely broadcasting how strong and tough we are. With this common model of living, we end up being the ones who lose out on anything new or meaningful ever coming our way. This fear and reaction-based way of life never allows space or vulnerability, it can never answer a question honestly, or hold the possibility of not knowing, or meet the openness of life in this moment.

The cure for this is to work on being teachable, especially from your soul. Allowing ourselves to notice our reactivity and fear, our sense of righteousness and certainty about "our way", and noticing that there is an energy to that. Then, rather than locking in, we allow ourselves to go beyond it through vulnerability and curiosity. Or if we do get locked into the same old pattern again, we allow ourselves to notice that we got caught – even knowing you are caught is awareness, and you can work with that. Whereas just being caught is not. This is how we begin, by noticing and letting that sensing of restriction Vs spaciousness begin to be our teacher. You might also find that as you go on you become more open to guidance from life, from books like this one, and maybe even a teacher, but please always let your soul come first and be your primary teacher.

4. Allowing intuition

As you become more aware of the spaces in yourself, between and behind your thoughts and feelings, your intuition will begin to want to guide you more and more. I'm sure you've done that thing that we all have, where you ignore the small voice inside you and have ploughed ahead with a plan or a relationship, you've convinced yourself or been very certain of a thing or a person and ended up crashed on the rocks. Well, that's never going to stop, but we can at least get on our own side by beginning to allow ourselves to listen and to even ask for guidance from that creative place inside ourselves that knows us better than we know ourselves. We can think of prayer and meditation as being ways of leaning into this space, or a way of offering things that are closed or unconscious within ourselves that we need to give back to life – so that we access the love and forgiveness that is the very nature of that space within. There is a beautiful practice called

Shenpa meditation that specifically helps us in doing this. It is included in of one of the meditations later on (in Signpost 5). It is a very helpful and healing practice indeed.

Little dust in their eyes

Let's close out this chapter with a tiny story from the Buddha's life and then there is a little assignment for you.

When Siddhartha was newly enlightened he went to sit by the river Neranjara, near where he was living in Bihar in Northern Bharat (India). As he sat by the river in meditation, a thought arose in him, which was the same core problem that you and I are reflecting on in this chapter. That though enlightenment is the simplest, most natural, and profoundly joyous and beautiful aspect of life, for most of humanity who are entrenched in certainty and conditioning, it seems impossible to show them the truth or to save them from the darkness of ignorance. Now, usually if you ask people about Buddhism, they will tell you that there is no God in it, and yet in the text that this story is related from, the *Ayacana Sutta*, the Buddha goes into deep meditation and feels the presence of Brahma. We will look at the difference between soul awareness and God awareness in Chapter 14, but I just wanted to point out that God as the oneness of all things, or Brahma, does appear in Buddhism. Buddhists choose not to see Brahma as a creator God in the Abrahamic sense. Questions of the existence of God of course are answerable by each of us by finding out for ourselves through our practice. Those who say they believe or don't believe, are actually saying that they don't know, and most are not prepared to try to find out by really giving meditation a go, or sincerely trying spiritual practice to see. The maintaining of righteousness and ignorance seems much easier. The Buddha realized that there was no point in his trying to teach anyone the truth as he had realized it, that there was simply no way through to people like the ones we have just described, and so it would be better just to live out his life in silence and meditation. Brahma knowing what the Buddha was feeling appears to him and asks him to look again deep within his meditation. The Buddha then sees that while there are so many who cannot and will not allow themselves to be teachable because their eyes are so covered with dirt, there are those who have very little dust in their eyes, who could soon come to their realization if he were to simply go to them and be with them. The radiant nature of his realization would bring them into the truth, help them be teachable, and so have their own awakenings.

After this, the Buddha rose from his seat by the river and, like every real teacher before and after him, set out to find those who would most benefit the world with their realization of the truth. The teacher, therefore, exists to be in service to others on their path of awakening.

PAUSE FOR REFLECTION

Please grab a notebook and pen or pencil.

Allow yourself 20–30 minutes for this investigation, so maybe grab a coffee and be relaxed.

Using writing or drawing or both, please allow yourself to accept this invitation with kind curiosity while you reflect on the following three questions:

- Am I teachable?
- In what ways do I get in my way with this, emotionally, mentally, physically?
- What am I going to do about this?

Please remember kindness and space as you try this exercise. I invite you to revisit these questions once every six months, or every year, to see how your answers change and grow. You can also use any of the questions we have looked at in this chapter as journaling, drawing or artistic prompts. Use whatever modality suits you best to bring more kind, curious reflection into your life.

SIGNPOST 2

THE URGE TO HONESTLY MEET YOURSELF

Somehow, by grace – and it is always by grace – we feel a sense that our lives are something more than what we have been told and conditioned into by the world. Something perhaps unnameable in you seems to be calling you on. Perhaps there has been something happening in your life that has brought the way things are into question. Maybe you have read a book or heard something within your religion that has penetrated somewhere deep inside you. You might have experienced a profound love or a meeting or an occurrence in nature or art. Whichever way it comes, something makes a hole in the concepts and thoughts of who we think we are. Often, it is suffering that punches a hole through the veil: a death, a loss, an illness, or a meeting with one's own mortality, or maybe we just wake up one day and know that what the world offers through its appearances and our acquisitions is not enough for us. We need something real to live by, though we may not know how to do anything about these feelings.

Or you might be one of those people who is born with a sense of their own soul that never leaves them. Usually, people like this just don't fit in that well with society, or they always seem to have the questions we've been discussing on their lips or in their bearing. If you are this type of person, you may have found your way, or you might still be seeking and reaching for a place to rest your heart. I'd say that every child feels this calling naturally, but it is more often than not quickly covered over by societal and generational conditioning as the established mechanisms of our societies work to turn us into a "someone". We are shaped to operate as a function of the society, rather than a human being moving through life fulfilling the fundamental goal of humanity and existence.

Whichever way it is for you, somewhere there is this urge. It will show itself in the drive to feel like you need to complete yourself somehow. In conditioned life, this is usually sought through status, money, relationships, power, or egoic completion. But it is this feeling that is trying to ask you to know the truth of your life. We've just been coming at it by thinking we have to become something. When you see through your conditioning in even the slightest way, you will find that this great desire asks you to know your sacredness just for who you are and invites you to be in that love that completely accepts you. There is not one person who does not have the urge to be whole and complete within them. Once we allow ourselves to meet this and not be in constant fear and reaction, we realize that we already knew this in our depths. This sense, when met with awareness, is the line that you can follow through all the voices and all the noise of the world. We will need it most of all, of course, when meeting the conditioned voice in our head that we have internalized and built to be so strong in its belief of who we are. "Why can't I just live my life? Why do I have to do this? No one else has to, and they are alright." This is where the heart comes in. The mind holds the voices of duality, whereas the heart is the bridge into unity. Life gets a lot easier as we begin to hear the voice of our own soul.

At first, we are most likely to try to ignore the urging of our soul. However, there is nothing we can do to run from it or hide from it. If we try to, we will keep looking for ways out: bargaining, denying, raging, addicting, shopping, working, trying to climb back into who we were before our questions arose. Thankfully the time comes when we look back on this resistance and foolishness with love for ourselves and the someone we tried to be for so long.

When I work with my students in classes or retreats, the way I teach is based on holding space so that they might find this space within themselves while beginning to allow themselves to become congruent with its guidance. Then there is no need to try to get them to accept or believe in anything. Once there is this natural receptivity, it becomes more possible to gently share guidance with them. Most importantly, it means that there is a more equal meeting which is self-propelling and that things cannot end up in the egoic messes that so many teachers end up in with their students. We have seen and heard of this so often, but thankfully there is some movement away from this now toward a greater reliance on authenticity. This is my hope for this book too. That it should meet you in this way and that you step into your journey with a taste of the sacredness within you. Then we might also have a bit of honest fun with things along the way, which is a much better way to walk together. This work is too serious to take too seriously. A lot of humour, forgiveness, and love is required. This is, perhaps, the second most important rule of the path, the first of course being: "Don't be an asshole."

FIVE RULES OF THE SPIRITUAL PATH (JUST FOR FUN)

1. Don't be an asshole.
2. Love and forgive *ad infinitum* (including yourself).
3. Authenticity and vulnerability are your real strengths.
4. The path requires tea and biscuits and often chocolate.
5. If anyone you meet in a spiritual group sighs, says they love you, and comes in for a four-minute hug – RUN

Only kidding, but not really …

For the remainder of this chapter, let's look at the first of what we might call the four dimensions of awareness, and we will continue examining the miasma of ignorance and misunderstanding that we began to explore previously. Only now, we will start naming things to see more clearly and give your sweet awareness a chance to start meeting them so you can better find your way. That is if this is the right way for you. It may not be of course, and that is fine. There are as many paths as there will ever be people, but as the Buddha said: "There is but one taste to the ocean." It is my hope everything here is very practical for you, and that you feel encouraged to look at how you can start working with this material in your wonderful life.

The four dimensions of awareness

The key to the whole journey is awareness. Rather than being a process of learning something as information that we can hold on to, it is imperative to understand that we are not making an externalized attempt at trying to embody something in an accumulating or "fake it till you make it" kind of way. So many commandment-based or precept-based practices are sadly taken with the attitude of wearing their guidance as rules or laws. Naturally, we strive to be good within the rules of our religions and so on, but we will often feel that we fall short. We can quite easily end up living out an egoic and controlled/controlling version of someone who follows the rules. Yet our intuitive sense of life can get so buried that we utterly believe this striving self is who we are. This is the situation for most of us in the world today, including many people who consider themselves to be on the path. It's not that the precepts and commandments are not trustworthy, but we have learned to wear them as masks rather than realizing and expressing their truth. Your innate human qualities, such as compassion, presence, empathy, not killing, and authenticity, are all expressions of your soul and your awareness. They are not concepts or constraints. Thankfully life keeps on turning up, trying to show us the bigger picture.

Over the decades of my own practice, I have realized that there are four dimensions to our awareness that act as the truest gauge of our progress on the path.

To paraphrase them quickly, they are:

1. Noticing delayed awareness.
2. Greater awareness of inner life, less interest in stories and drama.
3. Presence-based awareness.
4. Spontaneous awareness that is informed by genuine insight.

Don't worry, we'll be exploring these in depth as we go on.

Once you are aware of these dimensions, you will find yourself more able to learn and realize things yourself. Awareness will allow you to meet your own life with increasing love, honesty, and forgiveness regarding your questions. These four aspects of awareness are the most reliable compass I have found, and with my hand on my heart, I want to tell you that I would not have survived without them, nor would I be speaking to you now through these pages had I not encountered these truths.

As you work with the aspects, they will guide you to become more congruent with your own core of being. This process is the absolute foundation of the journey. Awareness is the very basis of who we are. Making a conscious choice about meeting your path as sincerely and as honestly as you can is essential at each stage because if we don't, things will just rise up anyway. If we don't meet things with awareness as they arise, situations tend to end up looking like they are happening by chance and will usually result in suffering. If we are not open to awareness, we will often find that the learnings and strategies we hold dearly will only work so far. We will try to impose them and the views stemming from them on ourselves and others to create a sense of control. They will also fail us completely when we most need them, especially when we face change, love, death, and so on. We then usually blame someone else or some external factor for things not working out. Our shift to vulnerability is what brings us into awareness, and hence the opportunity to live our human situations with wisdom. We also get to access real love, presence, humour and freedom. The increase of these qualities is a very reliable gauge as we make our way. As Carl Jung said: "Until you make the unconscious conscious, it will direct your life and you will call it fate."

The process we are speaking of always comes down to being more of an allowing than a making. Awareness has to be met with an attitude of allowing because it is already who we are. It is plain crazy to try to make awareness come into existence from a place within our thoughts, yet this is often what we try to do. Our conditioning tells us that we have to make something happen and that the mind is really in charge of everything. There is a common idea that we have to battle with our minds, destroy our egos, and break our way through to enlightenment. This just keeps us lost instead of guiding us home. To be sure, our thoughts can really help us in our shift to a more allowing attitude. Our minds are beautiful tools to have, but they only become genuinely beneficial when illuminated by awareness. Please understand that they are not to be silenced or got rid of. That is a huge misunderstanding that has crept into spiritual teaching over the years. Thoughts are not our enemies, but they are not awareness, and the mind is not an end in itself. More often than not, mind is a product of conditioning and an expression of our consciousness, both of which, as we are discovering, work a lot better when lit from within by awareness.

Please see these pauses for reflection as an invitation to be curious, kind and honest with yourself. The early steps of the path often seem to have an element of having to roll our sleeves up and dig in. Even on the level of our basic neuroplasticity, the initial work is naturally much harder when we begin because our wiring has been trained in certain directions. We need a lot of loving persistence at the beginning. On a simple physical level, this part of this path necessitates us having to heal the old wiring and begin encouraging better pathways. I'm honestly not trying to convince you of anything here. A life of meaning and spirit consists of turning up for yourself, and through space and grace, realizing things for yourself. Please do your own research around habit and neuroplasticity. No one is ever really wholly stuck. It's doing the work that counts. Later in this chapter, we'll look at some easy, effective ways to encourage rewiring.

You may want to take a break at this point, then come back when you've have had time to process.

PAUSE FOR REFLECTION

This is a practice to meet the first dimension of awareness. Rather than simply describe it, I want to try to give you a taste of it first so you will know it and realize it for yourself, and then we can discuss it.

Please reflect on a time when you had an argument with someone. One of those situations where you felt that you were really in the right. A relationship-based argument, perhaps. Whether you won the argument or not is unimportant, but what I'd like to invite you to sit with for a few minutes is how your awareness felt at the time of the argument and then in the days, weeks, months and even years that followed this event.

- What do you notice about your understanding of the event as time went by?
- Did it change over time?
- What happened subsequently to your sense of being right?
- Did or do you still keep telling yourself the story of being right to maintain your sense of what happened?
- If you moved to forgiveness, how long did it take?

- Was the relationship damaged or broken by this happening?
- How important was it for you to be right at that time?
- How important is it for you to be right now?
- Did you reach a point where you can't recall what was so important to argue or fight over?
- Did it work out that you came to see that things were not as you thought at the time of the argument?

Perhaps journal about these questions or go for a walk and talk with yourself in nature. We are not trying to find blame or shame here, they serve no purpose on this path, but I lovingly encourage you to meet and bring love to them if they do arise, and please get some support if needed if they are very stuck.

The first dimension – delayed awareness

Reflecting on your investigation, I'd like to draw your attention to your quality of awareness across the timeline you have been considering and how much of one's awareness can seem to lag behind our groundedness and our sense of being present. At the same time, you may have become aware of a quieter place or a stillness within yourself while observing your sensation. This time-lag effect and its qualities are the first dimension of awareness, and it is the part of you that can see that delay that is the edge of your more presence-based awareness.

The deeper place that is quietly beneath things is actually what a great deal of this journey is about. This space of awareness is present in all life and in all people, but we have been taught from the outset to live and identify with the more apparent strata. Our minds and feelings are so important, but the deeper awareness in us is all the more. We can go as far as to say that it is our deeper awareness that actually makes mind and feeling useful to us. Our conditioning through what we might call false consciousness places our lives in the time-lag through a certain kind of attachment and lots of stories and drama, while often laying down iceberg-deep levels of insecurity around our survival. This leads, as you would expect, to misplaced ideas of who we are and what we are here for and keeps us in fearful projection into thoughts about the future and past. It has also dramatically warped our sense of human purpose and potential. Just starting to know, even in the tiniest of ways, our deeper awareness while noticing our tendency of time-lag will begin to change your life and how you relate to so many things. Returning to this over and over again through your practice and in your daily life is the main mechanism of moving toward meaning and freedom.

Spiritual deafness

The delay in awareness manifests in many other ways besides the obvious reactivity and clinging it can bring. Something that used to cause me a whole heap of trouble in the past, and I see this in many others too, is that before what we might call the shift in consciousness, I was completely full of my own thoughts, judgements and criticisms of the world and people around me. So much so that I could not really even hear what people were saying to me. Have you ever tried to have a conversation with someone, and there seems to be a denseness to their ability to receive you? You might have needed to repeat what you said to them several times. You notice that whatever you say to them gets filtered and turned around to be about them or is always seen through a particular lens so that things are never met in honest simplicity. It always seems to turn to be about their opinions, reactivity and defensiveness instead. We often try to deal with this in people by walking on eggshells, never talking about the problem, or we find we become combative. Either way, we go around and around in duality, time-lag and separation.

The first dimension of awareness always makes things so complicated for us. Notice how it loves drama and how we mistake this for being just the way life is. Often we just don't feel very alive in the world, or we believe that we must work very hard to break through to being in the moment. The layering of objectification, projection and reactivity that we often face in ourselves and others means that we do not meet each other in our humanity. This dense quality is blind and deaf to everything that crosses its path. It can only relate from its own hardwired point of view. This was how I was, and maybe through this discussion, you can see aspects of how you have been at times in your life too. I didn't know when I was trapped in all of that how easy it is to move on from this state by dropping back into the quieter awareness that is beneath everything. This shift is the key that restores not only our ability to hear, see, understand, and even broker change, it also restores our humanity and our love in an instant.

Double trouble

One terrible tendency that we too often resort to is to double down on the false identities that we believe ourselves to be. This goes along with constantly being on guard to defend ourselves from seeming attack. This hardwires us into feeling that we are even more separated from life. We keep on doing this because we fear threats to our egoic identity, and because we want to feel that we are right, that we are the hero in our story, and that we are in some way special. It all adds up to a feeling of being separate from life, and to the darker aspects of our ego this is all that matters.

When we start working with the practice of taking a moment to hang back in our senses when this kind of tension and doubling down arises in us, we find that we can use it as an opportunity and doorway to enter the space of deeper awareness rather than going into the more separated state. One mechanism that I developed to help myself access deeper awareness in everyday life was that I simply started putting my hand on my heart when I was in situations that tended to pull on me. As I made this part of my daily life, I noticed that I could feel the energy under the surface when I was about to slide into reactivity or get lost. I even started to put my hand on my heart when I'd already slipped and had gone over in to that embattled place. Once I noticed that I was in the midst of a bad situation, usually an argument or being trapped in the voice of condescension in my head, I would put my hand on my heart and allow myself to drop out from speaking, while becoming aware of the sense of charge and righteousness. I found that I was able to come back to sanity and kindness really quickly. At first I used to worry that people would see me doing it and be critical of me, and I'd be shamed somehow, but then I realized that most people don't notice or care even if they do see you. More importantly, I was saving my own life by doing this, so thoughts of how I imagined others might be seeing or thinking of me were in fact tricks of my own false consciousness trying to keep me from healing and growing.

I'd like to offer you the hand on the heart practice if you should feel drawn to it. It is the quickest and most effective way I know of to drop back into the truer aspect of awareness that we've been talking about, to come out from our deafness, drama, and sense of war, entitlement and being put upon. Many of my students use this, and the results it brings are always surprising and remarkable. I still use it today and can't see a time when it will not be of service. It is so beneficial when talking with another person. Try it and see how you get along. As I'm writing this book, I'm periodically taking moments to put my hand on my heart, as I want to communicate with you the best I can because you are worth it. The hand on the heart is in so many ways the Swiss Army knife of being able to meet our deeper awareness.

More questions that help

As we begin to work with awareness and start seeing the time-lag effect and its resulting reactivity, fear, and inflexibility of identity, we start to meet some other huge questions which include:

- What is really causing this?
- Why do we continue to live in this way?
- What can we actually do about it?

As we have seen already, it is sometimes enough to simply ask the question. We don't necessarily need to dig deep and define all the answers. On an intellectual level, it can be helpful, but often asking the question is enough to allow us to drop into that space of awareness that we are talking about. It is that small movement back into ourselves, into our bodies and into our heart that is the invitation that returns us to the here and now. If we chase the questions too hard, we can end up defining what is going on as some kind of pathology or set of symptoms. The path of intellectualizing is alluring as it leads us to believe that we can outsmart our conditioning with our thoughts. This, too, is the false consciousness of conditioning doing all that it can to stay in charge of our lives. You will find that it will do anything it can to keep you from actually putting your hand on your heart and from being present in life.

Three of the most important words in any language

There are three essential words that we are terrified of. Together they are one of the most invaluable parts of our toolkit for having a life rooted in meaning, awareness and humanity. Shall I make you wait until the end of the book to reveal them? Only kidding. Here you go, they are: "I don't know."

Saying "I don't know" when we don't know is not a cop-out when it is said sincerely. In fact, it is the key to all knowing. The shift into the space and awareness that it brings, like our heart practice, allows us to access our deeper intelligence and our basic goodness. It is the most beautiful call to adventure because we can always follow up "I don't know" with the incredibly life-changing "but I am willing to find out". These are two of the great gateways to meaning and wisdom, to awareness and awakening. They are also the way to starting to see ourselves and others with greater love and compassion. They change the world. There is no science without them and no meaningful human progress without them. Yet false conscious conditioning has taught us that just being able to quickly respond with a smart answer or run rings around others with our argument or filibustering is what passes for intelligence so much of the time. We've built so much of our world from this approach. Consider the number of times you have seen a commentator on TV or a politician of any stripe use these two phrases and mean them. There might be the occasional one, but it will be a rare exception to the usual, I am sure.

Understanding false consciousness

It would be good to look at the mechanism of what really causes us to be lost. It is important to say that the time-lag and identification with false consciousness that we are discussing in this chapter usually envelops people's lives almost completely. Try as we might, there is little we can do about it in others. But your own movement into the heart and into truth and awareness is the key to the world changing by a factor of one. Your awareness is what will change your life and the world, though it won't be in any way that you can currently imagine or dream of. This waking up is what is most required at this time. This is what some call the beginning of the evolution of consciousness. Through it, we gain a meaningful choice of how humanity steps forward in this moment.

We are at a time when the survival of our planet and the life on it is not assured. There is indeed a strong impetus for us to shift, but we currently still choose duality and all that it brings. False consciousness is the cause of all the suffering we think of as a normal part of life. All the wars, insanities and iniquities in the world that seem like they have always been and will always be are rooted in this. Stepping into the heart of "I don't know, but I will find out" – into the vertical deeper dimension of your awareness – is the change that is most needed.

Let's look then at what false consciousness is, how it is placed onto us, and how its nature is to continue itself at all costs. You already know what to do to start moving into the reality of life, but I think it is essential to explore its mechanics with you. As before, and with everything here, you already know this, and this is to remind you that you know and invite your heart into the work.

What is false consciousness?

In a nutshell, false consciousness is the programming you have received from birth, from the sounds and the voice you learned to make in order to be fed, and to be taken care of, to the absorption of the models presented to you as what the world is. These come from your parents or the people who raised you, as well as the generational conditioning within your family line. The society and the worlds you adopt later as you "look for yourself" are also part of it.

"Forgive them Father, they know not what they do." It is vitally important that as best we can we don't choose the blaming and shaming path toward those who we see have laid this conditioning into us. Jesus's words are very important to keep to heart as we set out and throughout our lives. When he says this, he means that those killing him, torturing him and mocking him during the unimaginable human suffering of his last hours are lost in their false idea of who they think they are and their projected worlds. As your own realization deepens, you will find that negotiating how to be in relationship with others who are more bound to false consciousness than yourself will be a significant aspect of your work. Trying to persuade others of your truth won't change anything and only distracts your own journey. It is vital to remember that we were equally lost just a few minutes or days ago. Forgive them and yourself as best you can by coming back to the heart as quickly and as often as you can.

The strongest beliefs

Before the arising of questions, before the first noticing that we are out of presence and caught in the time lag of reactive time, we will wholeheartedly believe in the mind objects that we live through regarding the models of love, relationship, work, the meaning of life, national identity, modes of expression within society and family, and so on. We will believe that these things are who we really are. We may think that we need to become a particular something to be loved. That we have to speak a certain way to have a place in the world. Our body is not the right kind of body for the life we want, and certain kinds of people are our enemies. Perhaps we believe that we are only safe with those who look like ourselves or agree with us. We tend to create worlds with those who represent our norm, and we feel intensely that we must defend and fight to preserve these norms. As we move forward, it is of the utmost importance to ask ourselves if we have unconsciously imported this way of doing things into our spiritual seeking.

Modular living

Within the false consciousness way of life, we believe that the only way to have a better life is to get the right modules of the objects we believe in lined up in the proper order. We work and struggle to try to get our things in a row. "One day, I'll be just right, and then ..." And then what? We'll be loveable? The world will recognize how special we are? We'll find our true purpose. We'll get the sex we desire. We'll get the material trappings that will make us the somebody our conditioning says we should be. We need to live materially, and how we do that should promote the wonder of our lives, but what we are talking about here are the ideas we have that are primarily projections based upon the conditioning we have acquired. For example, we may get married in the hope of finding love and security. When we meet people, we unconsciously project our conditioning onto them, making them responsible for fulfilling our conditions, and all the while, they are doing the same to us. A lot of the time, we never really meet each other; we only meet our projections and conditions. Then, after a while, if things are not working – fulfilling our illusory requirements – we suffer, the other person suffers. Perhaps we let them go and begin the search for another person, and again the dice rolls. Around and around we go.

Looking at the religious, spiritual and yoga worlds, we see that this norm operates within our spiritual seeking too – if I am seen to be spiritual enough, minimal enough, vegan enough, yogic enough, humble enough, work hard enough, express my art or dance my spirit enough. So let us be bold and see clearly that what passes for our everyday normality actually leads us into greater and greater unconsciousness unless we meet it with awareness, then it can become our teacher.

Observe how we've also learned to approach concepts of overcoming duality with this same insane bent by believing that the opposite of two is one. The other side of division is actually wholeness, not one over the other. Thankfully, the light of life and truth occupies all the spaces we don't fill up by clinging to falseness. There is always a doorway in the present moment, through awareness, true intimacy, in the best aspects of family and being in nature. So, while the mind and ego will see what we are discussing as an insurmountable problem, there is always a way home again.

All this craziness boils down to a totality of belief in ourselves as a somebody, who achieves life through pushing into the false mind objects that we believe in and hold dear. These illusory objectifications get hardwired into us and are projected outward as an undeniable reality. Working with the brain's plasticity is an excellent first step in beginning to move toward freedom, but of course, we need to know that freedom even exists, to begin with. Remember that even the desire for fulfilment through false consciousness and mind objects is still the desire for wholeness, and although this desire is tinted by our perceptions and our programming, the great desire for completion is our essential nature, and its proof is in everything that we reach for.

Not nobody

The way out of being a false somebody is not to make ourselves into a kind of spiritual nobody. Transcending this duality is about realizing the fullness and wholeness of yourself. Awakening is coming to the full human expression of your soul through your ordinary life.

Here's a short list of some of the most common objects which are often most entrenched in false consciousness:

- Our models of survival in the world
- Our models of love
- Financial models
- Models of security
- Our models of belonging
- The models of our relationships, including our connection to self
- Our values and ethics
- The idea that we are separate from other beings and the world
- The cult of our individuality
- Religious and faith models
- National and tribal identities
- Certain aspects of sexual and gender expressions

I'm sure you could easily double this list.

One way of looking at your own objects is to perhaps think of your life as a room and the objects of false consciousness as the furniture in that room. We have a tendency to place our attention on the objects in the room. We might find ourselves wanting to change our couch. Our life might be better with a new TV. That rug needs to go, you might even be eyeing up changing your wife or husband for a new or 'better' model. The thing we usually fail to notice in our houses and rooms, in our lives, is that the most essential thing is present but not usually seen directly. We are aware of it because there is no use of that room or house without it. What we are pointing to is space. Nothing can exist without space. An over-cluttered room becomes difficult or unliveable very quickly, though we will likely try to keep adding objects into that room. Over time it becomes hard for anything new or vibrant to come into the space. This is only a metaphor but works quite well in trying to relate this. If our minds are full of mind objects, we can't grow and learn. If we are full of stories of pain, we cannot feel and heal. If music had no space in it, what would it be? This doesn't mean we shouldn't have a couch or a mind. It just means that without the greater awareness, all of our attention goes into the wrong place, and we are overfilled with things that are perhaps not really as important as we give them credit for. We might also find that once we become able to sense the space in which the objects exist, we can learn how to arrange them better, use them more meaningfully, or we might realize we really don't need these objects to be wholly ourselves, and we can just start enjoying the space outside of ourselves and inside ourselves more.

Here's a question that I won't answer but will leave hanging with you just for fun. If a house can only be built and lived in because of space, what happens to that space when the house falls down? Where does it go?

Are your parents to blame? Or society? Or your ex?

Certainly, false consciousness is a system that organizes everything it can materially so that it may continue itself, and indeed, the people who raise us and operate within false consciousness don't know any better. If they did, the world would not be like it is. But since you are the one starting to question things, you are becoming what Carl Jung called a transitional person, and it is this that needs to be the focus of your journey. Healing your psychology and learning about good boundaries is far better than going down the blame route. If your generational unconsciousness has manifested in violence, toxicity and codependence, then this is especially important to hold space for. It only takes one person to make this journey, and that person is you. Rather than looking to apportion blame, we might begin to turn to meet ourselves and who we are within these things. We have to lovingly own our lives and take responsibility for our lives wholeheartedly, come what may. As we heal, we may come to realize our own part in these things – again not in blame, but we realize that we've resisted learning to heal so as to hold onto a particular identity that seems to give us power in the world. Many things happen to us when we are young or powerless. Now, as you come to realize awareness, you also discover that you are not helpless any more.

Permission to heal and grow

All of us spend a long time looking for who or what to blame, but we eventually find ourselves asking: "Now what?" You don't need anyone's permission to live your life or make your journey of realization. You don't need the consent of those closest to you, nor do you need mine. But at this stage, I think the first of our "Five fun rules" from earlier really applies as we start to feel the urge toward freedom. Don't be an asshole, but do allow the voice of your soul to begin guiding you. If what you are doing becomes an identity thing in false consciousness, then you are not on a sacred journey; it's something else. Something that still needs integration. If you are truly hearing the voice of your soul, even if it is just the faintest echo, then the vulnerability that it brings will be both your trail of breadcrumbs through the labyrinth and your armour and light in the dark.

Celebration day

When you start to see the operation of false consciousness in your life and in the world around you, and as you begin setting foot on the path, it is indeed a cause for great celebration. Yet this pivotal moment is rarely recognized in our world. Be assured, however, in the depths of humanity, it is recognized and known. Your journey is the most important thing there ever has been and that there ever will be. It is the point of life itself. So, in celebration, I raise my cup of black coffee to you being a transitional person and your ever-unfolding journey of meaning and awakening. Here's to you. Watch out – it's about to get wild. You'll be taken to the precipice repeatedly through these early stages, but if your awareness is deepening and you are becoming more presence-based, you won't meet anything that you ultimately won't be able to handle as long as you allow truth and radical honesty to shine in you. Just keep the watchwords of love and forgiveness in your heart.

Blockages

There are a number of areas to look at:

Superficial thinking

There are several blockages that people run into over and over again at this stage of their journey. The first is that we try working too superficially. We often believe that we can somehow get beyond false consciousness by thinking different thoughts or adopting a strategy presented to us in a book or video or by a teacher. Sometimes we believe that we have already changed because we've read about something, so we feel we have it down by adding it to our intellectual knowledge and ego. We may reinforce this superficial way of doing things by adding an outward spirituality to ourselves, though it is usually quite recognizable in us by our performativeness and defensiveness and that old chestnut of forcing "our truth" on others at every opportunity.

Superficial spirituality and sudden change

This follows on from the above in many ways, but in this instance, we may sense the truth a little more clearly and then try to suddenly change everything in our lives too quickly. Our language, dress, diet, and the way we are with others suddenly are filled with the eager identity of this spiritual change. We try to rush ahead of ourselves and don't allow our soul or our presence to do the work of transforming us naturally. We shift to another mind-based identity, then we marshal all our energies to protect, defend, and try to live up to this within ourselves.

Searching for a club to join

Our third example again follows on from the two earlier ones, and is quite understandable, and is perhaps even what we need at the time. Though we do need to exercise caution. Often, as we feel the urge to grow, we look for our tribe – a group or others like you. It's natural to feel drawn this way, we are social beings, and the soul wants us to be in life with each other, to find a place of fewer boundaries and greater love and understanding. In the early stages of the journey, finding others needs great care. Many people and groups want to capitalize on you or take your innocence and energy to serve their ideologies or purposes. We have seen this repeatedly in religion and spirituality for as long as there have been records. On a personal note, I find myself wanting to reread Dante to see whether there is a special hell for those who misuse our spiritual innocence for their sex, power, money and status.

Hopefully, if you are searching, you will find circles of other genuine seekers.

Of course, there are many other considerations, such as family and societal pressure trying to stop your growth when it senses even the slightest difference in you. There's the inability to find trustable resources because we just don't know where to look yet, and there are the times when we feel like the whole world is quite mad, and you wonder whether it might be you who has gone bonkers. We could make a long list indeed.

The way through

One of the core messages I hope you feel drawn to is that just doing the work will take you forward. This has to be your journey, and I don't want anything for you other than your own true freedom. Your journey is your business and has to be undertaken in free will, which includes the freedom to make every "mistake" there is.

Relating to our blockages from earlier, it is easy to see with even the smallest amount of presence that a superficial intellectual approach is typically rooted in fear of being open to real questions. Questions such as: What is the root of the problem? How might I be contributing to it? These are unfathomable by us when we are lost in egoic identity. Any approach of truth can be shouted down, made illegal, persecuted, shamed and outsmarted. But the truth is always going to be the truth, no matter what we lay down in its way. We can spend our time and effort in learning a lot of information and perhaps even talking a good talk, but on their own, they are not the work of the heart or the soul; it is so easy to get stuck on the wheel of chasing symptoms and identities instead of honest reflection, awareness and proactivity.

The solution with all of the elements we are speaking about is not to reject intellectual learning, or our dressing up, or investigating groups and religions if they are helpful to us. And that question is the key: Are they helpful? Do they want our adherence or our freedom? So we can choose to base everything we do on seeing whether it is congruent with our deeper awareness or soul. No outward thing is sacred: only the soul of life is. Congruence with what is deepest in ourselves is the only accurate compass for our journey. We can look wherever we like, wear any clothes and dance any dance, but the only home we have is our soul and awareness expressed through the life and the body we have.

In terms of study and reading, I would encourage you to try to read or listen to what we might call "enlightened teachings" and genuinely trusted people's commentaries on the teachings. Allow your awareness to guide you. Try out everything. It is all for you to explore, but never be afraid to leave any group or party when your inner voice asks you to. How other people or groups respond to your desire to move on will tell you a great deal about their intentions. Every teaching should be giving you back to yourself always, even if you want to attach for conditional purposes that are still unhealed in yourself. All teachings should always guide you back to your life being your responsibility.

Societally, there is a place for bringing in structures and ethics and so on. We would not function well without them. We are not working that well with the ones we have right now. Consciousness and congruence need to be applied as we make our laws for ourselves and others. It is such a strange time on our planet now, where it is hard to know what is true from a mental or emotional perspective. So it is imperative that we treat ourselves and others with forgiveness, love and compassion.

My mum used to say: "Always keep a bit of something for yourself." Through our congruence, we do our best to stay as kind as we can in light of the blockages that we are discussing throughout this book, but always allow yourself to listen to your inner guidance and don't go against the voice of your soul as best you can hear it or feel it. However, if you do end up in a sticky situation, you may have something you need to learn from it. Don't get me wrong though, the situation or person may also have no lesson to teach you whatsoever. Being lost and making mistakes are often the most incredible teachers. Not the easiest at the time, of course, but how often have you found that something that seemed like the worst thing turned out to be the best thing that ever happened? As awareness deepens, we won't need to learn this hard way any more, but until we realize awareness, the hard way is life's standard method of trying to tell us to come home.

Remember that only you can make this journey. It is yours and no one else's. You do not need anyone's permission, though company and intelligence would be nice at the end of the day; however, the journey is yours, and by being so will benefit all. Your soul is your keeper and truest guide in all things.

Five tools to help you here and now

We need a few good reliable tools on our journey, so I'd like to offer you a range of things that may be of service to you whether you are just starting out or a long-term practitioner. The right tool for the right job is always the best way to get things done. Many of us only had a hammer that was handed down to us while growing up, and while a hammer has its uses, it's probably not that helpful for when we are performing heart surgery, which in many ways we are.

1. Knowing your life is fully your life
Perhaps the number one thing that will serve you best on your whole journey is to realize that your life is your life. This realization allows us to start to take 100 per cent responsibility for every area of our lives: our health, relationships, work, balance, finances, self-determination, family, and so on. Every moment of your life is your life. Yet so many people think their life is somewhere else or will be some time later. "When I have 12 million dollars", "When I get home from work", "When I'm in the right relationship".

As you can see, all of these stem from the internalization of particular training and beliefs that we have been conditioned with. Hearing that "every moment of your life is your life" will cause some people great weariness, a feeling of "I just can't do any more ... I'm already doing so much to keep myself together". We hear that our life and journey is ours and think that we have to do something egoically, that there is more effort we need to make. It is often less effort required around those beliefs and more space to hear your inner voice. We really can't do more adding to ourselves, so we need to learn the difference between "doing" responsibility and "being" responsible for our lives.

2. Admitting you have a problem and that you don't know how to work with it

The second tool is about having the guts to admit to ourselves that we have a problem. We may not know what love really is. We may be trapped in addictive or codependent relationships at home, at work, politically, in our religions and so on. We may be ignorant of what our life is for, or be feeling helpless around an addiction. We could make an endless list, but the goal here is not to point and blame but to acknowledge things so that we can heal and grow.

Admittance of a problem is not a step down or a humiliation unless we're meeting this from an egoic perspective. Much of the world is built on pretending that we don't have problems or pasts, so nothing much ever changes. Once we honestly admit that there is a problem that we've been living through, the space for awareness opens a little within ourselves. It's a little like that saying: "If you take one step toward God, God takes nine steps toward you." The wonderful Indian teacher Nisargadatta said: "The mind creates the abyss, the heart crosses it." When we admit we have a problem and don't know what to do, it releases us from feeling so trapped and lost, and this creates space for us to explore the possibilities of learning, seeking and even receiving help.

Admission is the beginning of becoming genuinely responsible and authentic in our lives.

3. Actively enjoying your neuroplasticity

On the physical level of the body, introducing new and novel experiences can help us quickly build new pathways in the brain. Even just four days of doing things even slightly differently can encourage new neural pathways to start forming. Establishing healthier habits for yourself is rooted in working with your neuroplasticity. Things like changing up your route to work, exercise routine, walking and being in nature, yoga, meditation, running, baking. All of these, when used with awareness, can help create space for healing and newness.

Your journey is not just a physical and chemical one, it is the journey of your soul, yet our bodies and brains are firmly part of the equation. I advise my students to bring physicality and fun into things and try to see their journey with a sense of adventure and curiosity. The kindness of being able to laugh at yourself is paramount.

I'm particularly fond of dancing as a way to begin freeing us up. We tend to try to think through our feelings to try to figure ourselves out. But with dancing, you can dance if you feel good and dance when you feel like dirt. How would you move your elbows and knees if you allowed yourself to do the "I feel like dirt today dance"? How would your elbows move for the dirt dance? Allowing even this little movement starts allowing emotion to process through our bodies. You might find yourself smiling, letting the movement go through your body. You might notice anger and passion as you start to come into your dance, and there might be waves and surges of feeling with the movement. With this type of emotional-integration dancing, we move into embodying our feelings. As we surge or quieten, we may find things have shifted and been transformed, and there is no more to say. We may even feel some compassion and better space in us for ourselves and our "dirt".

I invite you to put this book down and put some music on and have a try. Dance whatever your feelings are right now, good emotions or bad feelings, loneliness, or loss, or even numbness where we don't know what we feel. There is no need to try to name them. Your body knows their real names and where they live.

However you choose to work with your neural pathways, getting your wiring to connect in fresh and helpful ways is deeply effective. Throughout your journey, I hope you can see that there is one underlying word that helps with everything, and that word is, of course, love. We need to allow love into our life, into our adventure in soul and awareness. The difference between, say, putting your clothes and shoes on with a bit of love and presence in the morning, or just throwing them on with your head already in the car and driving down the street before you go to work is the difference between life and death.

4. Realizing there are no magic bullets
In over four decades of practice and three decades of teaching, I've seen too many people indulge the belief that they can beat the odds and some kind of magic will take place so that they can keep all their stuff and not really change too much while making their spiritual journey. As part of our becoming responsible for ourselves, we have to actively let go of the magic bullets idea or the wish that someone else can do things for us. If I could hand you what you need, I would. Any genuine teacher would, but no one can give you their wisdom or their realization. Please understand that you have all that you need already. You have your life, your heart, mind, soul, body and awareness. They are all that this is about. You are letting go of what is false and revealing the genuine nature of yourself. The old chestnut of "the only way out is through" rings as true as ever. Though I prefer the thought that you have to get in to get out.

5. Allowing meditation into your life

Meditation is a beautiful, natural vehicle that we can rely on for this journey. Beginning and staying true with a meditation practice that suits you and which changes as you grow is something that is available to every person. Meditation is not an add-on to our lives, it is a natural human function. We will talk more about meditation in the following chapter and beyond, but I just want to say to you that while it is utterly vital to understand that meditation is so valuable, it is not an end in itself. You do not meditate to become a good meditator; you meditate to become free from conditioning and falseness. Meditation opens us to the wisdom and awareness that is within ourselves and around us and leads us to the place in ourselves that is the home we've always longed for.

Wash, rinse, repeat

As your awareness is realized more clearly, you will find that it shows you that you can clean up the things that it touches. Awareness shines like a light into the corners of our previously darkened room so that we can begin to see what is there and how we can bring love to it. Depending on where we are on our journey, we can often be tempted to leave the things we find are broken where they are and keep trying to ignore them while tripping over them. Though at some point, as awareness steadies, we can decide that it is better to see whether we can repair and make the space of our lives more harmonious for the sake of expressing our souls through them.

Awareness opens the space in us, and then we can choose to heal, create, and become more whole, and this continues through the whole journey as a kind of spiral. The same sorts of situations that used to present themselves to you will continue for a time, but as you lean into awareness, you will find that you meet things with a little more love, presence and heart. This then opens up further new space, and then deeper old stuff will present itself for reintegration and healing, Wash, rinse, repeat. No one gets out of this process, though we can waste our lives and destroy the world trying to avoid it, but when we accept our journey and the curriculum of our human life, we can start to see the joy, beauty and meaning of who we are much more clearly.

Crossing (erasing) the border

Most people will not even begin this journey. Even if they do, most will spend their whole lives battling with false consciousness, looking for magic bullets and trying to get to "being" through "doing". This is really not a difficult stage to get beyond. It is only the belief in the false reality and duality that keeps things going. False consciousness is like the invisible lines of borders that we make in our minds and place onto the maps of the world. They are lines of social agreement that so many wars have been fought over. They are ephemeral identities that cause so much division, pain and death, and which seemingly continue without end.

We can build fortresses and checkpoints, create ideologies and arm them to the hilt, but that still doesn't make these borders anything more than an idea, for they simply do not exist anywhere but within our minds. Yet how many people do you know who can see past this invention? Would they, if you tried to discuss this with them, be able to do so without getting enraged or pushing an agenda about the need to control people, or how we must defend ourselves against other cultures and so on? So many of us cannot even imagine that there might be another way. A way that seeks first to understand and then to be understood. A way of awareness and compassion, going beyond our daily dualities, admitting our past and our problems with a heartful eye toward wholeness. Sure, it would take a complete switch around of all of our clinging to history so far, especially within our politics and our economies and their purposes. And it is just the same for each of us individually as we see that we've been living through false consciousness and its projections. We are not required to have guilt or add new beliefs. It only needs a shift of perception by the mechanism of awareness to move from being incarnated into those things to opening into that place where you stand in wholeness behind your own eyes. The place in you that is before the thoughts of your mind and the movement of your emotions.

SIGNPOST 3

THE INNER DECISION TO STEP FORWARD

Our third signpost is the decision within yourself to step onto the path and to find some practices to help you on your way. They say when the student is ready, the teacher appears. Perhaps it is also true of your path as you feel that sense of needing to move beyond the ruminations and feelings that often precede this step. There are so many offerings available to us, it is almost dizzying. So how do we choose? In moments and times when you feel less caught up and more in presence, you can perhaps set aside time to survey the choices you feel intuitively drawn toward. You might do this by journaling or chatting with someone you trust who is genuinely supportive of you – proactively beginning to use the urge to see your next steps and how you might equip yourself for your journey ahead.

In this chapter, I want to extend an invitation to you to explore a range of practices that I've found to be most effective in my own life and that I have seen to have been meaningful to people from every walk of life. We'll begin with three fundamental practices that are extremely helpful at every stage of the path. Later, we'll look at a method that I developed for myself at a time of great necessity, which I call "the path of ordinariness and upgrade". I hope that it will be of service to you and help you see how a gradual and steady sense of growth is possible, no matter your situation. Then we will close this chapter with a look at how meditation works and offer you the first of a number of practices to help you navigate your course as you move through the dimensions of awareness.

Three practices

Let's look at those three simple practices which will help you cut through the noise, no matter where you are on your journey. Whether this is day one, or you are an old goat like me, you may find that this is the right time for you to start working with them, or you may not come to them for many years. But if this journey is real, you will likely be drawn to meet these practices in some form when ready.

1. *Arya mouna* – noble silence

One of the best ways to allow ourselves to be in our true awareness and inspired by our intuition is to include some periods of silence in our days and commit to this as a daily practice. I'm sure you will be aware of the practice of silence within many religions, and you probably will have also seen it used as a kind of trope where we imagine a person adopting silence to cut off from life or to hide from the world.

In ancient yoga, there is a beautiful practice called *arya mouna*, or "keeping noble silence". It is generally one of the first practices adopted by anyone who sincerely wants to find their way into union with their soul. You begin by allowing yourself silence first thing in the morning for 30 minutes or so, which also means not looking at the news, phone, or putting the radio on. It doesn't mean "shushing" everyone in your household and demanding their silence, but rather we just allow for space and quiet. The reason for this is simple; often we jump into talk and ideas as soon as we wake. We grab onto things like social media, emails and the news and are lost in them straight away. We give them our energy and are pulled reactively by their triggers and demands. With *arya mouna*, we can instead allow ourselves the space to be based more meaningfully in our own lives to attend to what is essential to us from a more responsive basis.

Arya mouna is not a repressive silence; it is a space to tend to things lovingly. We can kiss our partners, love our kids, be with ourselves properly, make tea, prepare breakfast, do our exercise, meditate, do our ablutions and so on. For a short time, we just don't add anything extra. This type of silence will teach us everything about ourselves. It opens up love. It will show us our fears, allow us to access deeper wisdom and give our intuition and creativity space. It will show us where we hide, how our minds and emotions work. It also reveals the things and ideas that we cling to too tightly and so much more. As we deepen into it, it will also show us within a very short time the well of nourishment within our own being, revealing our compassion and help us better witness the wholeness of life.

As you begin to practise this, you may soon find that you want to keep *arya mouna* in other places too, perhaps driving the car with no music on, being in the gym without earphones, you might find you no longer want to go to noisy places as much as you used to. We don't ask for silence from the people and the world around us. Instead, we meet and allow ourselves to experience the silence that is simply under everything, and it quickly becomes a friend who guides and supports us. Then, we find that we can access our self-reflective powers and have a sense of who we are and why we are here. This kind of practice is something sorely missing in the world. It would be amazing if we were to teach this in schools, I always feel. We all would benefit so much from this.

2. Hand on the heart

This beautiful practice can be used everywhere and at any time, especially when you need a better sense of connection with yourself. The practice is to simply put one hand on your heart and to allow kind physical contact with yourself. I invite you to try this for yourself and see how it is for you. You can put your hand on your heart at any time, good or bad, when in public or alone – no one ever notices. It can be helpful when you are with people or in situations that tend to draw you away from your sense of being or when you are dealing with difficult things. Use it at any moment when you realize that you have to hold the line, or when you are out of sorts and need to come back to a better sense of yourself. It is a beautiful thing to use when you feel like you need some self-soothing. Try it next time you catch yourself entering into a situation that is argumentative or that has the egoic need to be righteous in it. You can use this technique as an aid within your meditation or prayer practice as a way to be grounded in the here and now a bit more when you need it. Perhaps when emotions are shifting, or when you are feeling stuck or needing to tend to yourself with kindness and compassion.

3. Contemplation of your death

I wasn't sure when to drop this one on you, as it can look terrifying, and it's far too easy to think of this as being morbid or morose or that this is to lead you into a place of nihilism. Rather than trying to scare you, this is surprisingly one of the greatest heart-opening and restoring practices there is. We can think of it as being like a shot of double espresso to wake us up. This ancient and classic practice is not about walking around, talking about everything dying all the time and losing hope. As usual, a sense of humour is vital with ourselves here. This contemplation on our physical mortality helps you to cut to the chase. Who are you? What are you here for? What is most important for you in this moment? What matters most in this relationship? What if this is your last meeting or moment with this person? Do you want to be here in presence and love, or do you want to cling to defending false conditioning? We squander so much of our lives away lost in things that are supposed to be important but that aren't worth a minute of your time or attention.

You can turn to this contemplation whenever you feel stuck or have a question about life, work, relationships, the meaning of how you are spending your time. In my own experience and in working with my students, I've observed that this practice moves us toward the heart, to a clearer and often more practical place of love. It cuts through fear, indecision and lets go of a lot of our castles made of sand. One powerful element of this practice is that it can also help us see how we can get out of our own way. It can help us see how we can contribute more meaningfully to the world, such as making a little extra food when cooking and giving it to the homeless person you pass every day. Being kind to the person serving you dinner or coffee. It takes you out from the need to be right to a place of seeking to understand. It allows for space so that you can be of service and provide leadership. Whichever way we are guided, the roots of this simple, effective meditation lead to the same place, a place of courage, soul, love, and presence.

The path of ordinariness and upgrade

Have you noticed how as a species we have a habit of trying to jump to the very end of things instead of making the journey the destination? We so often hear about an idea, then, without even reading the instruction manual, try to move to a place of acting as if we completely understand or perhaps even that we know better. If it does involve some time and effort, we tend to look for the shortcut, say that it's simply not worth it, or cling to defending our old beliefs. It's just fear of failure or of facing ourselves, of course. We do this, not realizing that this clinging on to the old state is the only thing that is any kind of actual failure. A striking example of this in the modern day is how so many countries don't acknowledge or admit their histories with any kind of eye to conscious change. Many go to the point of obscuring their history in any way possible to appear to be in a place of success when they are not. We often mistake culture for reality, and so it becomes part of our individual narratives too. A lie will always be a lie, even if everything has been rewritten and time has passed, and we have all forgotten the truth. Few of us walk in the valley of being willing to find out or even more courageously stay with the mystery of not knowing so that we might find some truth.

We try to become a somebody by assembling wardrobes of beliefs that we hope to stand firm on. Things that we hope will be enough for us to live by. We rarely question the actual value of the things we think we are trying to achieve. If trying to add things to ourselves worked, we'd all be "enlightened". There would not be any war or iniquity in the world. We would not be destroying the very home we live in and are part of. There would be certainly less personal and global everyday suffering. The types of ideas we are talking about can seem extraordinary, but our tendency to identify with them, rather than the genuine utility of them, stops us from meaningful growth. Awakening is not an idea; it is your natural state of being. Notice, I say awakening rather than being awakened. This is because awakening is not an endpoint. It is a continuity that eternally unfolds.

Human beings live on three levels simultaneously, our ordinary human level, the level of life energy, and the soul level. Though we usually tend to only know that we are alive in a more surface kind of way. Meeting the path of gentle upgrade with honesty helps you to begin to see that we have to honour our human lives, and as this more authentic way begins to help you access some space, you then start to see that we also live on the level of the soul. You might also be able to see that your uniqueness expresses from a deeper spaciousness that is before the soul that we might call God. This is only my preferred word for it, and I won't use it too much, but I will use it. Please feel free to put your own word there if you need to.

Earlier, we reflected on starting to move and flex your neuroplasticity to encourage newness and spaciousness in your life, allowing your spirit to shine out a little more. Our path of ordinariness and upgrade continues to build on this neuroplastic and soulful way of working. You start to understand that there is no need to become somebody other than you are. We have to let go of seeing ourselves as a problem or a pathology and allow for spiritual and psychological healing and growth to occur by engaging with the ordinary parts of our lives. Start where you are. I have seen so many people try to start from a place they imagine is closer to their idea of the goal, rather than understanding that where they are right now is the only place they can be. There are no shortcuts, except for putting your hand on your heart in the here and now and not resisting the present moment. I urge you to find the no-shortcuts route in yourself. Find the authentic, the loving and the true. It is such a bold step, and yet it is the only step. Trying to add a specialness to ourselves does not work. It kills us inside. It is your soul that makes you special and more than sufficient. It's why the universe wants you here – to be yourself in fullness.

Don't rush

We must not try rushing to an end place of imagined perfection. For example, if we don't like our weight, we might look in the mirror and curse our body, and then every trip to the gym is met with trying to almost hate our bodies into looking like the picture in our heads. The better attitude is to meet this journey with a sense of adventure, love and vulnerability. Decide to get a bit healthier, clean up how you do things, walk a bit more, enjoy the gym as being a place of embodied fun. Then as a side effect, our weight is no longer a pathology, we just live a bit better, and the results and happiness start to take care of themselves. We adjust what we are doing to work better, adapting as things work or don't work, so that we are continuously learning and growing, rather than taking a head-down, eyes closed, grimaced, self-hate-based approach. This method is also a perfect analogy for the spiritual journey and how things really work. As usual, please explore this for yourself. These words are just pointers. Without your confirmation, they are just words on paper and thoughts in our heads.

Our practice of *arya mouna* is so wonderfully helpful with this offering. It can help you touch the truth of your physical, mental, emotional and human needs, creating space as you naturally start to see the three levels of your life. Baby step by baby step, awareness moves out of the time-lag reactive state into a more natural and responsive place of presence that will lead you onward. Step by step, your daily life becomes more incrementally authentic, beautiful and meaningful, and what is perhaps the most significant and obvious secret begins to become more apparent, that your humanity is the spiritual path itself.

Areas for possible upgrade

Here are some quick suggestions that you might consider when exploring areas where you can make meaningful steps on your ordinary path. Please don't try to do too many things from the next few chapters, trying to add together a magic path and fill up all your time. Maybe just pick one or two ideas as you kindly step forward with yourself. As things begin to free up, change and growth become more possible in wider areas. Don't try rushing to the end with anything here. If you do, and we all do this over and over, come back to any real place of your sense of wholeness again. Forgiveness and loving humour will help you more than I can say.

One rule to rule them all

We never get this right, but we keep on unfolding. Awareness becomes more present, awakening continues unfolding, even after what we might call enlightenment (we'll talk about this later), and as you occasionally look back down the road you have walked footstep by footstep, and breath by breath, you will see that you have travelled far to a place we called "Here" and a time called "Now". I realize each thing we touch on here could warrant a chapter or even a book on its own, but I just want to hand these suggestions to you, so you can see what resonates for you, and I know you have the heart and intelligence to examine these things in relation to your own life. The key is to honestly do the work.

Your proactivity

Proactivity is the first step to anything meaningful in our lives. It means meeting the desire to move and grow as you can in this moment and then setting out. The baby-step approach is particularly helpful with engaging your proactivity, as it makes things attainable in a much better way than trying to jump to completion. Finding your genuine desire and engaging your proactivity is the underpinning of the whole journey, and you will not be running on empty as you go.

Your diet

Of course, this means water and food, but it also means everything you take in and fill yourself up with – news, social media, the types of movies and TV you watch, internet usage, opinions, stories and drama of those around you. Also politics, the kind of music you listen to, alcohol, drugs, medication. The things we consume, consume us.

This would make a good journaling session. Take a few moments to reflect on:

- What do you want or not want in your diet?
- What real step will you take with that today?

As you change things, it may leave a gap or a wound that you've been covering. What can you and will you do to heal that space?

Your relationship to your mental health

Mental health, just like physical health, can be improved and built upon. I'm not sure we can separate mental, emotional and physical health in reality. As we discussed above, your diet has a huge part to play in your mental health, as does your relationship to your body, emotional life, understanding your human needs, and so on. I invite you to explore how your mental health is not separate from your spiritual life, and vice versa. Healing your mind through *arya mouna*, meditation and embodied movement, and allowing for a change in our diet in the broadest sense of that word will mean a lot less buffeting on your journey.

Your relationship to your physical health, hydration and nutrition

Simple changes in your food diet and meeting your body's needs for hydration are so fundamental. There has been study after study that shows how these affect mental health and wellbeing, so there is no need to repeat all that again. But our conditioning around food and water is enshrined in us from the models we experienced when young. These are then often tracked into deeper grooves in us as coping mechanisms as we go through the seeming vicissitudes of life. Moving your body in ways that are natural for you to enjoy is important. Far from denigrating our bodies, the true sacred path shows you that your body is where you live. Loving care of your body gives your soul the only vehicle it can have for its expression. So please bring your attention here with great kindness and love and allow change rather than trying to force anything. Our tiny upgrades can go a long way here.

Seeing your family and work life as your spiritual practice

Every aspect of your life is your life. Imagining some ideal place away from our everyday life, where we can feel peace or think we are enlightened, is not a life. Only the areas of your daily living and loving will provide you with the curriculum that you need to follow to awaken into reality. Anything other than your own life is not you. This doesn't mean that we must stay in bad situations, but it does mean meeting every area of our lives with love, presence and awareness. The areas in life where we lose awareness and get hooked into identity rather than freedom can become our teachers. They can show us that there is something to meet differently from what we are currently doing. Relationships, work, friendships and all situations change how they look according to our willingness to meet them with awareness. There will always be comings and goings until we see that things are part of the flow of life, rather than being "things" in themselves.

Time in nature

Nature and our relationship to the earth is one of the best teachers we can have. All of life is our relation, but we have learned to put fences and walls around everything so that we feel our separate identities. Time in silence in nature regularly will teach you more about reality than any words anyone can offer you.

Your relationship to money

Money is one of the blind spots of our civilization, and it's not going anywhere soon. Perhaps we can't even imagine any other way yet, but there will come a time when the very idea of it will seem plainly insane. We have lived and died by our religion of money for so long. So, for now, if we are going to bring awareness to the subject, we must look at our use of it personally. I invite you to reflect on your relationship and honesty around money. Is your having it, or lack of it, a large part of your identity? What are you unconscious of in your relationship to money at this point? Do you believe it is somehow attached to people's merit? What does your relationship to money look like if you put your hand on your heart? Is it possible to personally relate with money and finance as part of the path? What can you do to allow it to be a more meaningful resource to bring healing and presence into the world in some small way?

Your relationship to the unconscious aspects of the culture you live in

In the same way that we are too often blind within our fiscal relationship, we are hugely blind to the fact that the cultures we currently live in are far from benign. Culture seems like it's the daily life we live together, but look at how lost and lonely we are as a species. Consider how far from consciousness we are so often. Does your culture assume certain norms of power, race, structure and so on? What would a culture based in even a tiny bit more awareness and sacredness look like? Consider how you might bring this to light through your action. Are we going to dream and wish while leaving it to others to dictate what the world is and how it works, or are we going to bring something forward from our light and heart?

Your belief systems
Our true beliefs are not the names of the religions we tend to say we are. Our cultures, our money, our sex, our ideas of power and race, our need to be right about things, the projections of our conditioning – these are our true religions. Who we are when we are alone with ourselves is the biggest mirror we have, greater than any words we say to others. Though our words and our accord invested in the status quo by saying nothing are also great indicators. We can work with each of these things by bringing our clarity of awareness honestly to them, and of course we have to be willing to give up the somebodiness we hold onto through them.

Your allowing of silence
We have discussed *arya mouna* a great deal already, but I hope you will come to see that this is because it is a key aspect of the path. It's the living silence in which we can communicate, love, work, stand in dignity and offer change and service to the world. Your examination of this core practice as you go on is central to everything we are trying to point toward here.

How you use your home
Your home, the place you live, is an outward reflection of your practice; you affect it, and it affects you. You can use your home, no matter how humble or grand, to help support your practice. Your home is a marvellous sanctuary and resource. Where we live can so easily become a prison of our own making, yet we can just as easily choose instead to orient it toward being a place that is safe and expressive of our values, our service and so much

more. It is worth reflecting on to see how you can use your home on your journey. It's not about the value of our property or even where it is, but rather allowing wherever and whatever we live in to be a reflector and supporter of our souls.

Your spiritual practice

Taking a regular reflective look at your relationship to your practice is also very helpful; we can fall into traps of becoming attached to certain ways of doing things so that they become part of our "somebody" religion again. Like all things, your practice must open and adjust to reality and awareness as things change for you.

The easy thing or the other thing?

There are limitless areas where we can find spaces to upgrade. The list above is just some suggestions to see whether anything catches your attention. One amazingly accurate way to know if something is calling to you is to notice that invariably there will be one thing that will look easy, and one thing that will have a strong charge of perhaps fear around it. You can witness your mind saying: "No not that one, do the easy one." Guess which one is going to help us most?

Two engines for real change

Each bit of space that comes as we allow change through the areas we've just looked at leads us on to more possibilities and opportunities. As a way of starting out, it is good to have these tangible things to focus on. As you move through the dimensions of awareness, you will find that you begin to become more stable and grounded and more present in areas where you would have previously been reactive or less conscious.

Here briefly are two seemingly small-looking tools that are in truth, real vital keys to aiding your growth. They look small, but they are each a lifetime's practice. I'd say they are enough of a path in and of themselves. They will take you through anything and they are the fastest bringers of movement and change there are.

1. Keep your word to yourself

Learn to keep your word to yourself in small, realistic ways with the material we have just been looking at. Sticking to your practice time, looking after your health, and doing what you say you are going to do for yourself really counts. Unless this is in place, we might think that we keep our word to others, but actually, do we? Or are we just chasing meaning, approval, love, an end to loneliness or some kind of energetic exchange? Keeping your word to yourself means becoming a real friend to yourself. It will teach you all about how you relate to others. Learn to give your word and keep it to yourself, and choose at the very least to have a win/win situation with yourself throughout this life. It is the difference between believing we are at war in the world and knowing why we are here. When we have our own back, and our own heart, we find that life has our back too.

2. Tend/tender

Life can so easily look as if it is a series of battles. Popular culture lays this down as one of its myths from the get-go. We feel we have to fight for our lives for everything or at least join in with the story of being ever stressed, strained and busy. I want to invite you to look at eight terrible words for a second: "'She lost her five-year battle with cancer." Just feel that in your body. How many times have you seen a line like that? What if the line went more like, "She tenderly met her life by engaging with the traumas and blockages that had led to cancer and lived for five years after her diagnosis with a deep sense of love, connection, healing and freedom"?

We are taught to fight for everything, for our work, for belonging, for money, for our country and for our identity. Having and not having are drawn as dualistic lines, over which we are supposed to fight and struggle to get from one side to the other. Even the sacred path is often rendered in these terms. What if your real work was for you to tend all the areas of your life as if you were a gardener learning through plant lore how to nurture and build your soil, as you raise your garden? Speaking and singing to your earth and crops by keeping your word and bringing loving awareness in the hearts of your family, work, your practice, your relationships, your health and nutrition. How might that feel to you? The idea of tending your life. I feel that tend is one of the most beautiful words that I know of. It allows for presence, grace, healing and wholeness. These are just two simple offerings that I wanted to share with you with an open hand. Out of all the ways of following the path we can take, I honestly feel that they might be the most important aspects of the whole heartful journey.

Meditation – the art of washing the dust from your eyes

In a book like this, you would assume that meditation would have been the first thing we talked about, but we've waited until now because, as helpful as it is, meditation is not an end in itself, and we really needed to lay out the ground of what we are actually working with. Meditation is the most beautiful and natural human vehicle for change and wholeness, and, when used properly, it can help us cross the stream of illusions and false consciousness. It quickly moves us into the space behind the different layers of our perception so that we may access our sanity, dignity and awareness, rather than flailing about at the level of our stories and the perceived difficulties we feel we face all the while, hoping for the best and trying to play to win. More than being just a solution to ourselves as a series of problems, our meditation practice quickly becomes a trusted space and ritual that helps us access love and healing. It is one of the main ways we can start to know our deeper awareness, and it is a profound way to spend time in the sacredness of life. This is all by degree, but if we commit tenderly to ourselves with our meditation, things will change. I often give a warning in classes, saying: "If you don't want to change, please don't learn to meditate."

Let's quickly look at the two most common meditation paths and investigate some of the blockages associated with starting to meditate.

PAUSE FOR REFLECTION

Grab your journal and create a list of your life's dimensions, your roles and responsibilities. For example, you might write: yourself, your health, with your partner, home, work, family life, your sexuality, your spiritual practice, how you use your time, and so on.

Spend a few moments writing and considering each area with authenticity and kind-hearted awareness:

- Where is it that you usually get stuck or give up?
- What do you need to do to drop back from the false conscious version of yourself to allow movement?
- How can you bring love and kindness into the areas that seem closed?

Step-Forward

For each area, write down in no more than one line what simple small step you will take today. Then keep your word to yourself and do these things today. Don't be tempted to overreach, overwork, or be performative or optical. Honest and kind are the only things that count, no matter how tiny the step may look. To facilitate real change quickly in your life, save your list, and repeat the last part of this exercise daily for 42 days. Repeat this whole exploration every couple of months as your awareness opens, and things grow and change. Baby steps are the fast track into life.

Focus-based practice

Meditation tends to fall into two strands. The first introduces us to using an object of attention, such as focusing on the breath. This is helpful because we might be caught up in reactive thoughts or lost in false consciousness, and the process of focus allows us to begin gathering into awareness. However, it is very easy to misunderstand the word focus and make a stick to beat ourselves with. This mistaken idea of what focus means also takes hold in the belief that we need to force our minds to be quiet or create a particular type of feeling, and then maintain that by being very concentrated. However, all this will do is make you ill in the long run and build neural pathways and grooves that stop you from moving toward the freedom you desire. It has also long been known and is now being demonstrated through a number of studies that, done wrongly, these types of practices can lead toward a greater sense of separation and egoic identity. So understanding and working with these practices in the right way is paramount.

Many people cannot meditate by using their breath. Often people who have suffered trauma, for example, will trigger into difficulty or panic when trying to focus on the breath. It is surprisingly common, in fact. If this is you, please don't take it to mean that you can't meditate. What we may not realize, because they are not talked about as much, is that there are many other objects of focus that we can use besides the breath. Breath is the most common focus for many meditations because of its roots in the popular Buddhist practice known as mindfulness. However, there are practices available to people from every religious tradition, so we have a much wider choice than we might think. For anyone who doesn't feel comfortable focusing on the breath, I tend to guide them toward more embodied ways of practising and using broader awareness-based meditations like feeling the life in your body or hearing the space between the sounds. I myself cannot meditate by resting on the breath, so you are not alone.

Regardless of all that, what focus-based meditations do,

when used in the right way, is act as a rudder to take us to a place where we hopefully start to see the wood for the trees somewhat better. We find that we have a choice between being lost in things and stories, and being able to be in more wholesome awareness with life and how things flow. These preliminary practices are perhaps most helpful when we are located in the first dimension of awareness, and we are just starting to look at those pesky questions about the meaning of our lives that keep popping up.

The direct path

I honestly feel that most people can enter their journey in a deeper, more meaningful and more straightforward way than through the focus-based practices if they will just allow themselves the small but radical vulnerability of dropping the "somebody" mask a little. We might call this route of meditation the direct path. All practices and yogas eventually lead here, as do all religions (and sciences) when met with an open wish to know the truth. I guess you might call this way of working the fast route, but in saying this, there is nothing wrong if you are a slow-route person. They are both in truth the same route because we can only be where we are. The path flows from the place you are right now.

Direct practices are usually much clearer about why we are here and are generally less wrapped up in their concepts. You will find that these practices are always hidden in plain sight. They tend to reveal themselves when you are ready for them and not before. It is even possible to be working with them and not see the deeper truth of what they are. The direct path, or the path of awareness, asks you to step into life by allowing and opening to what you really are. This is the process of discovering what is natural in you, no matter who you are and what your situation seems to be at this moment. The direct path shows us that this very moment is the basis of existence itself.

When the time comes, you will find that the path is right at your feet, right here in this moment where it has always been. All that it seeks is to take you home, like a beautiful friend walking right next to you. It is closer than that even. The direct path is intimate in a way that there are no words for. Only poetry, painting or music might be able to hint at the space of what we're trying to point at here. The direct path of the sacred doesn't pretend to be other than it is to capitalize on you or your life energy. Rather than asking you to believe you are free as long as you hold to certain things, the direct path actually gives you freedom, which is not something we are very used to in our world or that we see represented much at all. It does not seek our agreement. This can be confusing to us for a while, especially if we are still trying to add spirituality to ourselves rather than aligning with what is essential.

Every tradition has its direct-path practices, and I would invite you to consider continuing following your tradition, if you have one, until such time as your awareness naturally has no more use for that vehicle. Try not to worry when its time starts to end – transcending and moving on into new life is a chief signifier of the way.

I honestly cannot think of any tradition that does not have this side within it. Perhaps the underlying feature of each is that each has arisen out of the necessity to answer the two questions we began with. Each seeks that we may know reality, and that we allow ourselves in our naturalness. Each practice in its own way and language points to you knowing your soul, to knowing God by knowing the heart within your heart. Each just says it differently. As our brother Jesus said: "The kingdom of God does not come with observation; nor will they say, 'See here!' or 'See there!' For indeed, the kingdom of God is within you" – *Luke* 17:20–21.

There are always two sides to each faith, including the faiths of science and atheism. There is the label version or orthodoxy, and the path of realization or knowing. Jesus, like Krishna, Buddha, Lao Tzu and the others who came before him, and those who have come since his time, remind us that it is through "knowing the kingdom" within our hearts for ourselves that we enter the house of truth. We must drop our false consciousness and be humble to what is within the deeper heart. We can do this at the very least within our practice and begin to let that wisdom teach and shape us. So in a very long-winded way, this is what is meant here by meditation. I know the word can mean many other things, but on the path of your own ordinary and beautiful life, this inner urge is the thing that you can feel all the time under your wishes and desires. We can each enter into this right here and right now, if we will but allow it. This is what is called the direct path.

Blockages

To be honest with you though, I have found that both types of practice are often presented by people who have not really met the path for themselves. There's a strong egoic tendency for some to read a few books or do an eight-week course of some kind and decide to call themselves "teacher". A form of being a "somebody", of course. This is often reinforced with inherited wealth, doctorates or celebrity and various combinations of. We fall for it so often; I don't know why.

The tendency to reduce sacred practices to materialistic and seemingly rational things is also a great problem. You'll find said somebodies or institutions calling their presentations of the path "the such and such method" or "_____ yoga", sticking their name or branding on it. Never, of course referencing where these practices are actually from or what they are really for. The origin of this materialist approach, which is in both the East and West now, goes back to the dark ages of religions operating by the sword and the still ingrained tranches of patriarchy, dogma and religious, cultural, and racial supremacist beliefs and so on. A lot of schools and universities have yet to begin addressing these difficulties, never mind committing to heal from them. These strands can also spill into the spiritual-teaching world too, along with a strong entitlement of cultural appropriation operating to the same ends.

The way through

We don't have to fight the whole world with this stuff.
They are of course part of the air of the hegemony of
false consciousness that we breathe and project through
unconsciousness. As ever, you need to reflect on what we
are discussing for yourself. What kind of consciousness or
awakening can we have if we have not met and healed these
broken ways? Deep down, we all know the score, but it takes
real courage, love and vulnerability to look within ourselves.
We think we will have to carry shame if we dare to look at
these difficulties, and perhaps for a time we will, but admitting
the problem honestly is the only door to healing there is.
Shame can be healed and will pass – an open heart will always
find its way beyond shame into the clear light of day.

Regarding teachers, there are some really genuine people
out there. Perhaps the best way forward with this is not to
worry too much, but always listen to your deeper heart when
choosing a teacher, and don't be afraid to move on if there is
not a space for your full heart in what you find.

The integrity of our practice communicates everything.
The area of ignorance around teachers and teachings is a real
tough thing to bring up, but that's the journey, to go there
and to bring awareness, to look for "dis-ease" within ourselves
and to bring love and healing there. We are not trying to get
anyone else to change. Each of us is making our own journey,
and that is enough, but we must also be unafraid to call out the
dangers we find so that we can support each other when they
are obvious. Once we are more grounded in our hearts, we can
see that the areas of patriarchy, divisory ideologies, relativism
and cultural appropriation and so on are real pain bodies that
we are suffering from on the personal, national and global scales.
The authenticity of our practice and the movement into real
awareness is the challenge that is needed to bring change to our
old entrenched broken systems. The truer our path, the more we
stop feeding the energies of unconsciousness by incrementally
unplugging from these cancerous systems of resistance.

Embracing our freedom can be scary at first because it is actually a real thing, and we are not prepared for it to be other than a fiction that has kept us going in hope for as long as we can remember. Freedom is not a concept or something outside of ourselves. When we say freedom, we don't mean egoic and narcissistic free expression, the likes of which hold so much sway in the problematic areas we are looking at and have become constituted within the dualistic nature of politics these days. Freedom means knowing at your core the reality of what is. In our modern world, we tend to call this knowing awakening, and it is vital to understand in whatever way we can that this is a loving path but is also a radical path that brings great change to ourselves and the world.

Allowing discovery and change

Your practice needs to be allowed to grow and change as your awareness grows. When you start working with your mind and emotions, anything that is unconscious or held down will head for the surface and ask to be met. This is quite natural, as is the sense of being confused as to whether you are getting things right or not. Strong emotions are bound to show up and move through you as you start to open up a bit. We need a maximum amount of patience, forgiveness and tenderness throughout the whole journey. Our cultures have trained us to usually try to get beyond or bypass the things that are under the surface.

Your ego will certainly play hell with you for a while when you start meditating. Don't try to force yourself into focus or try to squash things to get past them. Instead, allow yourself to drop into the awareness that is within you in whatever way you can. Let's not try to fake it or try to get it right. Then you will find that this little step inward is the key to everything. It is from this movement that we can then acknowledge and meet whatever is coming up. These things have to come up as they need to be met. This is such an important distinction. Awareness and heart are always the answer, and they are very different from head thinking and force.

We have a real addiction to believing in the primacy of thought in our cultures. "I think therefore I am" has become a truism that does not serve us at all well, but we keep on with it regardless. What if we tried "I am therefore I think" – how does that feel? Thought is not wrong, your mind is not your enemy to be beaten, but as you will see when we look at the models of meditation that I want to show you in a moment, mind and thought are not what comes first in a human being. Thought is a product of consciousness, and so for this very reason it cannot access either the creative or the sacred. Our minds serve us much better when we use them as the wonderful tools they are from awareness. Chasing thoughts while trying to get them to behave in a certain way will have you lost in an endless knot forever. Accessing awareness is the step out of the tangle toward the tangibility of your own life again, and your mind and thoughts will thank you for it.

Two views of meditation

I want to share with you two views of how meditation works, and then we'll try a beautiful meditation to help you develop into your awareness. These are not "my models". I'm just noticing and sharing what I see with you. The way I think teaching works best is that it is like one of us seeing an apple falling from tree in autumn and saying to the other "Hey, look at this phenomenon".

View 1 – the structure of a human being

This first view of meditation is best presented as a diagram for you to reflect on (*see* page 82). It moves from your outer being to your inner being, but your existence is not linear – it is concurrent across all the layers, and spontaneous. In other words, you are happening all at once, all the time.

Above: Simultaneous aspects of awareness available to each human being

Both soul and God awareness, as well as awareness and life energy in the body, pervade every layer of your being, and so are available to you at any time if even the smallest inward shift is allowed rather than "created" or "forced". Created and forced attempts at the movement inward are rooted in ego and false consciousness and always lead to pain and further conditioning.

View 2 – a timeline of practice and expected effects

This view of meditation unfolds along your own timeline, not by days and months and years necessarily, but more by your honesty and integrity with yourself as you practise. There is an element of establishment through the years of practice, but you can often meet people who have been practising for 30 years and there's no hint of more compassion or less anger in them. Then you meet others who are just a few years along and their lives have changed entirely for the better. So time is not the best indicator, but it is a small factor. Integrity is everything. The timeline unfolds like this:

- **Normal state without meditation or spiritual practice:** Experience of life being in things (false consciousness) and/or identity primarily located in the frontal lobe. You may have an occasional sense of presence, but it seems tied to luck or beliefs.
- **Beginning to meditate:** Awareness of thoughts and feelings not being all that you are. Identity begins to move to the centre of your brain and the compassion and empathy centres. New neural pathways begin to form.
- **Occasional flashes of presence:** Sense of wholeness, joy, dignity, oneness of life. Less self-identified. Greater sense of your life as a whole. Urge toward healing and contributing to the world.
- **Presence begins to establish:** Beginning of realization that you have a choice in all things in your life between "being in" things or being "in being". You experience more balance and wholeness. Creativity and intuition increase.
- **Presence established more of the time than not:** Occasional direct experience and beingness. A clearer sense of your soul. A truer sense of sacredness arises. Meditation is maintained as it cleans away the daily accruing of negative build-ups, while nourishing you with its periods of more profound access to presence. Creativity and intuition significantly increase.
- **Awareness is realized in its third dimension (presence-based):** Life knowledge moves to be more rooted in wisdom. Fuller realization of the importance of your ordinary life and the choices you have. You are more deeply aware of the sacred dimension of being in daily life.
- **The fourth dimension of awareness (spontaneous) is sometimes available:** Meditation begins to give way to grace but is maintained as a practice as it gives you an anchor in the world.

Please note these views of meditation are only trying to point at something that there are really no words for. Everything here can be said another way, and perhaps more accurately. However, I hope they show you that at every step of the way it is accessing the space of awareness that leads you home. This shift is the key to not being lost and incarnated into things. Most of the world resists this tiny vulnerability, and we look for something to hide in, to fill up the time. The truth is that the space of awareness is available to everyone right now, no matter who you are or what your life, or this day, has been like.

Cling-ons

Once we take that inward step, we have to be careful not to fall into the trap of believing that we should try to make an effort to make this state or experience last forever. The stage of trying to hold on to our practice is something we all have to go through, so please try to remember your sense of forgiveness, humour and self-deprecation when you catch yourself doing it. The practice is always about this moment, the one you are in right now. We worry so much about later, the future, the next moment. When those future moments come we find that they are also this moment, and that we always have had a choice about how we arrive here.

Meditation is not for everyone

Please hear this. Meditation is not a panacea for all things. For around 25 per cent of people, especially those suffering from depression or who have trauma in their background, meditation is not the place to begin. Finding healing through time in nature, embodiment practices, and accessing space are recommended first and always. I don't want you to hurt yourself by thinking "no pain/no gain". Real meditation and yoga will never cause you pain or injury, but they will always ask you to meet the pain you have yet to heal and integrate. This can seem like a terrible burden from the pain body's perspective whose only goal is to continue our suffering, often by trivializing and normalizing it, or by bringing in shame to sustain itself. All genuine meditation paths, religions, and yogas will never cause you pain, and the same is true of any real teacher.

Look from your spirit

There are many who say what sounds like the right things on this path, but I ask you to reflect on what your spirit knows about the people you meet, including myself and this book. Please try to see from your place of deeper sight and intuition rather than with the ordinary mind and emotion. Check and recheck as much as you need to, but forgive yourself if you get things wrong. Forgive the teachers and the books too. Everyone alive is a human being, and the goal is not in getting things perfectly right. We all get things wrong so often, we sometimes end up becoming wise. The direct path always invites us to strike a balance between healing our psychology and removing the blocks to the more direct loving awareness that is who we truly are already.

Gathering awareness practice

You can do this practice in any formal meditation seated posture. Or, if you are ill or unable to sit, you can use a chair or lie down. There is nothing inherently spiritual about sitting a certain way. Though the ritual of taking your seat, as with all rituals, creates a space for you in which to practise.

You may want to do this practice, and the other meditations later on, book in hand so you can follow the prompts, or you might choose to read through the directions and then let yourself move through the stages guided from within. Both methods will help you to build self-reliance in your practice. Don't worry too much about getting things right; we are working with principles of awareness, not following train tracks made of rules. Meet this practice in a way that feels right for you.

Allow around 20 minutes for this practice once or twice daily, though sitting up to one hour can bring a much deeper sense to things, but please note – how long we sit for does not buy us credits, and if you catch yourself in that game, just laugh with love.

Gently gift these words to yourself as you take a comfortable sitting position.

Allow yourself to become aware of your natural breathing. Don't take over your breathing, just allow your awareness to notice that you are already breathing and have been doing so since the day you were born.

Become aware of the feeling of the space of the room around you with your felt sense.
Not thinking about the space but just knowing it.
We can only sit here because there is space to do so.
So, gratitude for the space to sit.

Let awareness feel into your feet, legs and lower body.

Let awareness travel up your spine.
Relaxing your back, shoulders, arms and hands.

Let awareness be aware of your neck and head.
Face softening and being easy.
You can close your eyes if you feel you need to, but if you get lost a lot in thought or emotion and lose your sense of being where you are, gently keep your eyes open, and look 4 or 5 feet in front of you.
We are not trying to stop thoughts or feelings. Just begin to notice that you are aware of their energy.

Aware of your chest and heart.

Aware of your abdomen, the movement of breathing in your body.

Aware of your groin, and your reproductive and excretory organs.
We leave no part of ourselves out.

Aware of your whole body.
Aware of the breath.
Aware of the space of the room around you.
Aware of yourself sitting with all this awareness within the space.
Let go of naming, reacting or labelling.

Aware of your inner organs — just the sense of them.
Aware of how your body simply feels right now.

Take a moment or two and just allow yourself to be here.
Allowing yourself kindly to be still rather than making yourself be still.

Treating all this as a little adventure and discovery with a sense of enjoyment.
Meet this moment with awareness and freshness.
Letting mind and emotions be.
Not tumbling after each thought or feeling.

Bring your awareness to the sounds you can hear without naming or labelling, just hearing.
Notice you hear the sounds and can simply let them be without reaction.

Notice too you can hear the spaces between each sound.
Be aware of sounds and spaces with equal weight.

Notice how the awareness of sound enters into your consciousness directly and how thought and feeling come after the flow into consciousness. Spend a few moments enjoying this.

If you get lost, just come back to the sense of the space of the room, the sense of yourself, the sounds and the spaces and the entry into consciousness, don't try and get back to where you were and don't get lost in any blame when you get lost, just re-enter the practice like this. There is no getting it wrong or right or perfecting this. You are just gathering and deepening into your natural awareness, beginning to recognize its sensation within you.
We now repeat this process with each sense taking a few moments with each.

Bring your awareness to the feeling of your clothes against your skin and notice the inflow of sensation directly into consciousness.

Bring your awareness to the light coming in through your open or closed eyes.
Notice the deepening core of awareness that you are.

Awareness of the air in your nostrils in the same way.

Awareness of the taste of your mouth and follow that in too.

Take a few moments with all the depth of awareness that you are.

Being aware of the space that your mind is taking place in.
Notice the movements, spaces and attachments of thoughts.
Not trying to change them, but just noticing the mind's energy from your awareness.

Aware of the space that your emotional sphere is taking place in.
Notice the movements of feelings, the spaces and attachments as energy.

Not trying to change anything, just noticing from awareness.

Now let go of all efforts and simply rest in your deep awareness.
Be aware of your body and all that you are.
Recognizing how this feels for you.
You are aware of awareness itself and how it feels.

Perhaps you feel a little more present, or you notice that the mind has quietened, or the emotions are more open with less pressure.
Perhaps you have a sense of yourself more fully as you, something new yet original.
You are aware of your basic innocence, yet this is not childish.
A sense of something more eternal or fundamental.
Recognizing this deeper feeling without effort for yourself.
There is no thing to attain here.

Resting into:
Your body breathing.
The space of the room.
The space within yourself.

Your belly soft. Your breath natural. Your face relaxed.
Feeling present and alive in this moment.

Please continue sitting for as long as you feel like.

To bring this practice to a close, notice that you are perhaps more here than you were when you began, and so there is no need to come out. You can just decide to close the practice and move gently into where you want to be next.

And so, this meditation ends.

Go slow if you can

Please do go a little slowly, and perhaps allow yourself a period of *arya mouna* following your practice. Tend gently to things. Grab a cup of tea or some food if you have time to. We don't need to be too precious, but it is good to give ourselves a bit of time, so we might choose to not suddenly pick up our phone or look at news and social media.

Our practice means we have begun the incredible journey to coming back to life from giving all the false consciousness and its energies rent-free space within ourselves. So do allow a few moments to honour this. Then we move into our day, simply living our ordinary lives and taking the benefits of practice with us as we learn the truth of who we are increment by increment. Signpost by signpost for ourselves.

PAUSE FOR REFLECTION

Here are three fun questions for you:

- How do you think you will use your growing freedom?
- How does the world look to you from here right now?
- How can you be of service today?

Revisit these questions from time to time on your journey and watch the answers change.

SIGNPOST 4

MOVING FROM REACTION TO RESPONSE

While the path we are laying out together here may appear to have linearity to it, it is, in fact, nothing like a line on an XY graph at all. The directionality of healing and awakening seems to go all over the place until it is simply realized. Even then, things are not a done deal. There is always much coming and going that we have to navigate and live through.

But in the early days, it's more often than not a case of some days we'll be up, some days we'll be so lost, and some days we have a real sense of "This is it". Which is usually then followed by more of the up and down, and then some round and round. Yet, if we can gently start to bring awareness to this movement of our own attachments and reactions through our journey so far, we see that things are tending to move slowly around in a spiralling way. The gathering awareness meditation from the previous chapter will help you start to see from that place in you that is sometimes called "the witness", which will help you understand your actual location within all this movement.

We find that we will meet the same old personal and worldly material time and time again, but if our journey is a true one, then we find that things that we once considered impossible to navigate are met with less much reactivity and a greater ability to respond. This new space often means that older unresolved stuff starts to turn up within our sphere, so you hold to your practice with kindness and see that these things are here now as they need to be met, healed and integrated with love. It is vitally important to learn what it means to stay embodied and in your heart throughout. As we discussed, you'll start to see that this process goes around in a spiral – deeper or higher each time, a crash here, a crash there, and onward and heartwards as we learn presence.

Natural and spontaneous

You are naturally and spontaneously becoming less reactive. So the inclination to take time to understand and respond more cleanly begins to emerge in you from under all the old layers you used to believe were your personhood. This awareness begins to lead you on with greater ease. Not to say that it is easy, but our idea of what suffering means will begin to change, and this gets much more pronounced as you realize the presence-based dimension of awareness more.

You will find that in many areas of your life that compassion, proactivity, action, and even meaningful silence start to become the basis of your responses. You notice that perhaps there is a touch less me, me, me in your talk and a better sense of self that doesn't look for attention in the same way as it used to. You look at others and perhaps don't quite jump to the same judgements and stories you may have previously. Better discernment starts to appear, and though you can possibly see the way someone is behaving egoically, you also feel a clearer regard for their soul. You recognize the roots of their false consciousness as being the same as the ignorance in yourself that is slowly starting to be left behind. This means that you start to have greater choices in your relationships and connections with other people and the world. You might also notice that your strategies for living become a little more malleable.

We must be careful to watch out for our old attachments getting hold of any growth we make, and just keep returning to that balance of heart, mind and awareness. Ego will get hold of anything and try to make a somebody for us. "I'm an aware person now." One way to have a good laugh at oneself is to say those funny in-the-head ego voices out loud but to raise the pitch like we've been sucking gas from a helium balloon. You might like to have a try at this method while you are reading this. It might make you laugh at the very least. Everything we are talking about in this first half of this book goes strongly in and out of focus until we reach a certain point with the following two dimensions of awareness, which we will look at soon. Try not to worry too much if some days you feel that you are in a good place and other days you feel like you have utterly lost it. Be reassured this is par for the course.

A funny thing

One really funny signifier that often shows up at this stage is that we start to make more trips taking things to the charity shop or thrift store. As we subtly begin to get a taste of our real lives, we find that we start to feel less like living through the things that we used to try to add to ourselves. Maybe we identified as an avid movie watcher, or a reader, a person into gadgets, or we love our sports team, and we know every score for a hundred years. We may be a collector of certain things. We all look for ourselves in so many places. However, once we get even the smallest taste of awareness and truth, we find that need to add to ourselves in this way starts to decrease. Actually, this is a big signifier. My big thing with being a writer was to be a really big buyer of books, wanting to be seen as being well read. Books are actually a great joy, as is being good in your field, but they, or anything we own, do not make us who we are. Once awareness starts to become clearer, we find that we need a lot less, but also, we can enjoy the things we really love more, but in a less attached and needful way.

A tripping point

I have seen many people make the error of trying to suddenly go totally Zen and minimalist at this point. As if rushing to get rid of everything will somehow lead to a more profound spirituality or quicker enlightenment. I've also seen many people go as far as trying to deny or get into punishing and abusing their bodies for holding them back. This syndrome is often concurrent with a denial of basic life needs like love, intimacy, sexuality, relationships, connection. You have probably met this person. Everyone except them (or us if we've gone down this blind alley) can see that this is just another ego-building thing. Another identity that they (we) are trying to use to be a special somebody. I beg of you, please don't rush to get rid of things or yourself, but don't hold onto them too tightly either. As you unfold into the truth of your life, things that are not who you are will just start to fall away from you, and you might find later on that you still like to play those old Led Zeppelin LPs and have a bit of a dance.

Things go away on their own

You will naturally find that your tastes start to change. For example, many people begin to question their diets and what they're eating as they meet a rising sense of wanting to cause less harm to animal lives and the planet. There is often a healthier desire to use food not only to fill up but also to begin understanding its medicinal and nutritional properties. A big question that always arises at some point is how we spend our time – drinking, going out to bars, the way we work – we may wonder what the point is of going after what we thought were our goals. We could easily discuss each of these at great length, but there's no need. The roots are always the same – we have attachments and conditioned beliefs about things that we believe make us who we are, which then gradually change to a desire for something more meaningful as awareness dawns within us.

I just want to remind you that a sense of allowing change, seeing this all as an adventure, and reaching as often as you can into kind curiosity as things come and go, is a far better path than the one of worry, struggle, gripping, or rushing, because we think: "This change will lead me home more quickly." Honestly, I have seen uncountable numbers of beautiful people living tortured lives and suffering with no real advancement or healing available to them because of this tendency. The path of freedom and awareness is both gradual and sudden, and you can never quite tell which is which. So let's stick with the foundations of kindness and love, and no matter what, we'll be on the right track.

An example of change from my own life

One real surprise for me many years ago was how I came to let go of alcohol. The question of alcohol comes up a lot with people as they start to move to congruence. I was quite a big whisky drinker back then. Single malts from Islay, if you don't mind. But my life had shown me quite clearly that the forms I'd been living through could not and would never satisfy my soul. Things had got to the point of completely falling apart around a decade ago. I was a lost soul at this point. I mistook false consciousness for myself in those days. Fortunately, things fell apart so completely, I had no other place to go but inward as a last-ditch attempt to know some truth. I had no choice but to start meeting myself with radical honesty and love, and so I'd begun to work on healing deep childhood wounds that presented themselves as what we call attachment disorder these days. I used to mistake that horrible intensity for my model of love. Love only existed in someone outside of myself, so without it, I was no one.

As the path began to teach me, I learned to keep coming back to being, to meet each thing with healing and love and kindness as best I could each day. My habit at night was to crack open the whisky and have a home-sized double.

One night I opened a brand-new bottle and took a sip, and something in me said you're done drinking now. It simply didn't fit in my mouth or life any more, and I knew it was true. The truth has a particular feel that I'm not sure there are any words for. I got up from the couch and, taking the bottle, I walked across the street and knocked on my neighbour's door, who was a fellow connoisseur. I handed him the bottle saying: "I don't drink any more, so I'd like you to have this." There was no effort, no idea of giving anything up, and no attached identity to even the letting go, now I simply don't drink. I tried a whisky again a year later and could only manage a sip – it was gone. The same process happened with watching TV, collecting movies and music and so on, all effortless. They just stopped being meaningful once I started living from my own life.

You will likely notice other things once you start moving into the deeper dimensions of your awareness, such as the dualistic and abusive nature of the news and politics or how we believe that stories and drama are the basis of relationship and so on. Once you start to see the nature of these things, you'll just drop them. Until then, we sort of know they are not true or good for us, but we keep on trying to find meaning in them, often making excuses for them so that we don't have to let them go. This is very much like someone caught in a narcissistic codependent relationship. In fact, considering duality as malignant codependence is an excellent way see how duality works on us.

You will rise to meet it

One matter we need to discuss before we move on, as there are a few things that will begin to happen at this stage, is that all these changes will continue throughout your whole journey in more and more subtle ways. It might seem like I'm telling you too many things, but from here on out, they are essentially the same things coming around again to be met at deeper levels as your stability and access to your heart grows. As you unfold more into life, there will be traps here and there that are more specific to those "stages".

What you do with all this is part of your journey; it is all grist for the mill. For each thing that seems like a blockage, there are an infinite number of benefits that will arise as you learn how to drop back to awareness and soul. This will take as long as it takes. There is never an end to it. However, if you have felt "the ground of being" within yourself, then there is nothing really to worry about now, or at any point of your journey. The arising of wisdom will begin to outweigh the clinging to beliefs more and more as you allow congruence with the light within you.

The second dimension of awareness – clinging less to dramas

We should talk about the second dimension of awareness. At this stage, we still have the time-lag factor going on, but it is beginning to decrease. As a consequence, you will find that you are clinging less to stories and dramas – the need to maintain the sense of righteousness that once seemed life-and-death important also starts to have more space round it. At times when you are in nature, you will likely find that you will experience greater expansiveness. You might also feel this sometimes with people you are close to. You find that your heart desires to share itself a little more in certain situations, and it's likely that you will be looking at the objects of false consciousness within yourself with more curiosity. At this stage, there comes the clearer sense that you are more than just your thoughts, ideas, successes, failures, relationships, money and so on. Most importantly, your sense of yourself starts to be less egoic and rooted more in actuality.

As things develop, you might find the impulse to be on your own more. Withdrawal from the surfaces of dramas and waves of conditionality is quite a natural feeling, so is not wanting to be around people as much as you used to. You might not necessarily withdraw on an everyday awareness level, and it's not a rule that you must, but perhaps things begin to register as discomforts or a sense of being too much for you in some way. At this level, there will likely still be some tendency to blame the world or see other people sometimes as being the problem, but this gradually passes as you move into deeper awareness. This period can't be outsmarted by good intentions or thoughts, but it can be met with wisdom, and as much love as possible for yourself and others.

What we call the world and culture is largely the unconscious interplay of reactions and conditioning that has formed into our systems of society, business and governance. And it's not just the political and economic aspects of things, but almost everything that is relational. As we move through the stages of awareness, we will start to notice and understand the parts we have played in all of this. However, we must heal the tendency to jump to blame, tempering things instead by allowing for meaningful change to occur within ourselves through our practice. Most change fails to happen in the world because we just won't allow it to. Clinging to and defending our old unconscious models is a huge part of how we do things at this juncture of the 21st century.

"Why don't you?"

As your discomfort with unconsciousness grows and forms the desire for a better way of life, you might find that people around you start telling you that you have changed, that you've become strange. They will question why you don't want to hear their stories or be part of things you used to. "You used to be more fun." Or they'll say: "Why don't you want a drink?" or "You used to love meat." You know the score. For a long time, we will try to explain things to people in the hope of communicating what is going on with us, but we ultimately find that we can't really transmit our experience.

I want to offer you a gift. Please just translate it into your own words. "Give them back to God, and then give yourself back to God." I read these words many years ago in a remarkable book by Melody Beattie, *Codependent No More*. This doesn't mean "throw people away and set yourself apart as a special or spiritual somebody". Instead, it is an invitation to notice how we get caught in our projections of what relationships are meant to be from the viewpoint of false consciousness. We can see how we try to hold onto them and how these cords ensnare us. We acknowledge that we are holding onto this energy for dear life. Then, without fuss, we allow ourselves to move into the heart space, into awareness. We find that we can open our hand and let that energy just rest there, letting the other person be – giving them back to life, to God. Then we do the same for ourselves and let ourselves be too. This process is truly a lifesaver, often a marriage saver, and a brilliant path to freedom for ourselves and the others in our lives.

A time of goodbyes

Some people will leave you as you go forward, and you will leave some people, and they may not be who you thought would leave. When we begin to look less for our meaning and existence in others, we start to feel our presence within ourselves. We will begin to see who our friends and families are beyond their conditional ideas. As the grasping within us eases up, we start to discover that we are more based in love, not fear. The desire to be more open and be with each other grows in us, but many of our friends and family won't see this. Any change in you can cause others to push more for their old models as that is where they feel safe and identify as who they are. Just remember we were doing exactly the same thing until not so long ago.

It is not an easy stage at all, and we have to keep meeting any ego attachment within ourselves repeatedly as it fights to create righteousness in ourselves. Ego often wants to make us the hero of our own story, "We're awake, and they are not". Try not to worry too much. I know how hard this time is. We have to lean into love and know that each person is on their own path. Any real shift in awareness in us causes a change in the world's energy, so your increasing opening will bring those who are a little more open in themselves into your sphere, or at least encourage them on a deeper level. It also tends to bring those who want to put you back in your place and reinforce their world vision as being the only one that is right. Thankfully one side effect of healing back to oneself is that our boundaries begin to operate more naturally rather than from reactivity and mind. Still, there will be some bumps and bruises for sure.

The compass of natural morality

A natural sense of a more genuine morality begins to glimmer in you. Rather than living through our given or adopted creeds so much, we start expressing what we might call our virtues. This is a wonderful sign that this path is for all, no matter what religion or non-religious background we might have. Again, this increases further as the spiral journey continues, becoming more and more naturally grounded in those essential qualities of enlightenment: kindness, compassion, empathy, awareness, right action and so on. They will come and go, of course, but there is no need to push into them.

Interestingly, as we go on, we become very aware of how uncomfortable it is for us to go against our virtues. This uncomfortableness acts as a wonderful compass once we start to recognize it. You don't need to give up your religion or science to follow your path. The direct path is so wonderful because it enables you to sense your religion's true religion through your inner guidance system, and we learn that things will simply change because they have to.

Blockages

It is easy to misconstrue much of what we are trying to discuss as saying "Just do your own thing". Materialist spirituality has long traded on this kind of "own thing", and "your vibe is your tribe" enshrinement of personal ego and narcissism as a way of trying to capture us. The modern spirituality, meditation, mindfulness and yoga of the past 60–70 years has been particularly rife with this. It's easy to understand why after the religious restrictions of the past and the desire for freedom coming out of that time. We want to be free and unopposed. A lot of this desire for egoic freedom energy is very much in play in the modern day and has become bound up with identity and late-stage capitalism, but it is far from any actual form of freedom and often tends toward tribalism. It has firmly become part of what is first offered to us when we become interested in who we are spiritually. We can quite easily get drawn into spiritual materialism and spiritual bypassing if we don't hold to our own council through our early days.

The search for a "tribe" can lead us to taking on the trappings and outward look of what the spiritual is meant to look like, saying the "right things", talking and believing things a certain way. Two killer aspects of this type of modern spirituality are the beliefs that we have somehow gone beyond all the world's difficulties by choosing spirituality and that we just need to stay peaceful and silent, and that not being judgemental of others means anything goes. This false approach abdicates the responsibility of having proper discernment based in awareness and humanity. It allows for suffering and hatred to grow very quickly and continue in the world as we layer "spiritual" reasons over why the world's problems are nothing to do with us. All spiritual bypassing is always about fear, ego and hiding as a default status. We fear being useless. We fear being nobody. We fear being visible. We fear standing up, and so cover our humanity in these rags. Spiritual bypassing makes us feel like we are all separate and not part of the family of life. It believes that it is far easier to appear to be something and somebody rather than meeting our own heart, admitting our frailties and sense of uselessness and unknowing. It fears having to open its heart to other people. It can't look another person in the eye and call them brother or sister unless they are part of its tribe. It pretends that it is above all the sufferings of duality and misses the mark of meeting life through life. Add all this together and we end up with a handmade prison cell in our own personal hell. It involves so much energy and resources to maintain this way of living, and all the while inside the false identity we are cut off from life, fearful, and there's often a braggart trying to cover over our imposter syndrome. You can sadly go far like this, right onto the world stages of power, the guru halls, and the bestseller lists with millions and billions in your bank account, but what good is all that without your own heart and soul?

We've got to get ourselves back to the Garden

This energy has driven a great deal of our history. If we dare to look under the very clear trap of duality that lies behind all such outbreaks of polarization, we find that it is always mistaking duality for reality that underpins all the horrors we visit upon each other. It's the broken belief that overcoming duality is about "one side" winning and the "other side" disappearing. We can't see the disharmony, ignorance and false consciousness involved in such happenings.

Duality in every form is never about the movement inward to awareness, never about going beyond false ideas of separation or oneness. Meaningful change involves a remembrance of being part of the family of life. Then we can work on the transcendence of our broken generational inheritances by being brave enough to meet the duality and separation together as a loving family. We need to give up our masks, our need to have our way and win the prizes that the world has told us are so important. We are not here to be separated into winners and losers at the game of life; we are here to add our individual colours to the great tapestry of being. To be in the heart space together in the great "I don't know what to do, but I'm here" gives us the chance to go beyond this warring way of doing things, to go beyond the spiritual bypassing, the performativeness and false impartiality that allows for the ever-deepening horror show.

It seems we human beings need a sense of purpose higher than ourselves to align with. Otherwise, we can fall into terrible places of fear and control and much worse as a species. In this very moment, anyone, no matter who we are or what we have done, or had done to us, can turn back to our heart, turn back to God, to living awareness, and start walking along the path home. Let this be our higher purpose, not the false ideas of success or winning the duality game. We all fall over and over again, but life just wants us back. Healing ourselves and thus the human family of our disharmony and dysfunction by allowing awareness to be a choice will enable us to meet and transcend duality in consciousness and love. Thus, we can address the problems of our day, and the past, through admittance and reintegration rather than living through the polarization of limited identities and entrenchment. Imagine if we would just shut up and sit down in *arya mouna* for a little time together every day and then have the courage to allow movement from there. Maybe we could put our hands in the soil and plant a vegetable garden or break bread together as a way to begin.

Noting the presence of the pain body

There is one major thing that perhaps you will start to get more of a sense of now, that these days we often call "the pain body". An example of the pain body is that thing that arises in us when we visit family, say, at Christmas, and within a few hours or minutes it reduces us to being like a four-year-old or a teenager having an emotional tantrum. The pain body can also manifest as being a silent, tense and inwardly turned tightness, so much so that we have no sense of space or possibility at all. We will look at this in the next chapter, but I wanted to mention it now as it may be on your mind. We've saved it for a bit later on as it is much easier to look at and bring healing to, from the third dimension of awareness, which we are also going to look at in the next chapter.

Three more little blocks

There are three more things that we may encounter now, so let's meet them in one little section here. Compared to pain-body stuff, they are nothing to worry about, but they do affect us. Perhaps, in some ways, they are like rays emanating from our darker ego.

- **Trying to convince others of your progress:** We might want to show how spiritual we have become and try to tell others where we are up to in our development because it feels important that we share our spirituality, which leads to ...
- **Pontificating:** Not only do we want to be seen in our new guise, we suddenly have all the answers for everyone else's lives. "If only they'd listen to me." Be assured that there is little way of avoiding this ridiculous stage, so hopefully we can just have a good humble laugh about it when we get a bit further along.
- **Thinking you are somehow doing this – sliding back to a doing rather than being:** Yes, we have some real growth, but then the ego gets hold of it and says: "It's me, it's me doing all this – I'm so special." We have to discover repeatedly that this aspect of ego can make a stand on anything. Once it gets hold of us, we think that we can somehow guarantee our outcomes by pushing further into it. If, or rather when, this occurs it means that we have not yet recognized how grace needs to be part of the equation and that it is the key to everything.

104

These very typical slippages are easy to notice because, as we slide back into this sense of being a special somebody, we find that the beauty, joy and spontaneity of life vanish somewhat, and things like our meditation practice start to feel like a chore or an inconvenience. We might have a run of good meditations. Then we start thinking we can have a good meditation at will, kind of like: "If I put this dollar in the slot, I will get the soda that I want." Anyone can easily slip into this materialist way of working. The key to noticing that we have slipped is to be aware that we lost the life and spontaneity of our practice.

The way through

As you might see, this period of the journey is often fraught with confusion. Don't worry. If you have tasted a genuine desire for meaning and healing in yourself, then no matter what happens, things will always come back to present you with your path again. This offering is available to us in every situation at every second. No matter what you have done, even if it is the worst thing in the world and you have landed in jail, or you got caught up in some mass hypnotism that exploited your fears for its own gains, or whatever, there is still, and always will be, the possibility of the movement back into awareness available to you.

Concerning the more problematic presentations of the path we've just been discussing, the draw to seek a tribe as things change for us does not need to be avoided. It is lovely to connect with others on the same journey. But, as ever, always consult your soul. We can't live fearing mistakes. If something is a mistake, we will learn from it, and if it's a good place, then it's a good place, and we will learn from it.

Suppose we find ourselves part of something that really goes away from our wholeness, then we just have to be honest with meeting that energy in ourselves that makes us susceptible and manipulable by these kinds of forces. When we admit our problem, we can access space and the possibility of healing. When we remain unconscious or deliberately try to stay ignorant, history will repeat itself. The ego always seeks agreement. It wants us to join its ranks and to add our voice and energy to it for its continuance. Your soul sees the one life in all things and so doesn't need to exert egoic pressures. There are good people seeking change, and of course, there are genuine teachers and teachings, but you never have to join anyone's club or present yourself as an image of something. This goes for what you are reading here too. Always take the time to check in with your soul and keep a little something for yourself while you are at it.

It seems to be getting faster

The transformation and transcendence of old limitations start speeding up from here due to your beginning to move out of time-lag awareness. It will sometimes seem like things are going too fast, and it can feel overwhelming and frightening. If you experience this, try to see that you're just rushing toward the present tense out of that old past-and-future-projection way of living. As things arise, it becomes clear that we will need to meet and heal the pain body and come into a loving relationship with any trauma and unconsciousness that we are carrying. This sounds like such a big thing, but it is the honest meeting with our stuff that is the true gateway to our freedom. We can choose to allow gratitude and kindness to be present as things arise to be healed, knowing that we are on the way home by doing so.

End of part one

You'll be glad to know that most of the heavy lifting should start to ease up from here, as you start to feel on some level that you know where you are, and you know where you are going. We have two huge areas still to look at as we go on from here, but these are more about honesty and awareness than we might think. I had to go through a lot of the stuff we are talking about here on my own, but you don't have to. One of the main reasons for writing this book is so that you might know in some way that you are not alone on this path. So many things on the path, especially the movement to awareness and healing, look too large and challenging from outside of their actuality, but they are not because love really does change everything.

I want to invite you to take some space here. You deserve many cups of tea, and perhaps some chocolate, or your equivalent.

See you over the page after you've had a rest.

PART TWO
HOMEWARD

SIGNPOST 5
A CLEARER SENSE OF CHOICE

As we move into the third dimension of awareness, which we'll discuss in a few minutes, let's take a look at our next signpost, which is that you begin to lean into realization rather than holding to beliefs. You will find that you have an increasing ability of choice in your life and how you meet the world. Meaningful choice is rooted in being able to be in awareness and presence in the situation of the moment. Even if you are caught up in the dualities of a situation, you start to notice you are lost, and so you can decide to come back to awareness. As you recognize false consciousness more for what it is, there is likely to be both a greater sense of possibility and burgeoning freedom. You will also have a real understanding of how much work there is to do, which might feel overwhelming to you at this point. Happily, now, you will find yourself with more moments of feeling spontaneously and deeply alive, and less caught in thoughts and stories based on projections of the future and past. You will find that you are more present in the here and now.

So few people are actually present, no matter what they try to tell you. This is not a judgement. Remember that we were all equally lost not so long ago. Thankfully things will be beginning to seem a little clearer and less out of control to you now. The period ahead is usually marked by a dawning series of insights into your own life, especially around the things that need healing and integration. This process never really ends, and we must talk about the continuously unfolding nature of awakening later.

Things might not be that clear yet, and there will still be a part of us that isn't sure if any of this is real or not. A lovely supportive practice is to read accounts of enlightened lives and others like ourselves who have also walked the path. Not for comparison or to compete with them, but to access voices of companionship and sanity along the way. Much starts to change now if you allow it, and you might find that as much as you would like, there is no one you know with whom you can discuss what is happening. Don't be discouraged. The guidance and voices you need will turn up as you need them, not because of any spiritual mind trick, but because you'll be more available to them now. They are all around you.

Over the next few chapters, as well as looking at the signposts ahead and the blockages you may meet, and the ways through them, we will also turn by turn look at two of the deeper aspects of difficulty within the human experience. We will look at the pain body and we will look at an area that spirituality often seems to bypass, which is trauma. Both of these are vital to bring awareness to, not just for the sake of the sacred journey, but to be a complete human being.

While we have talked about these things earlier, pain body and trauma tend to operate in a more deeply rooted and unconscious way than false consciousness does, and so can be harder to see. I felt there was little point in tackling these subjects in depth earlier, as it's not until we start realizing the third dimension of awareness more properly that we can do anything truly significant about them. Although, you may find that in many ways you have to go right back to the beginning over and over again while you learn about and begin to heal and reintegrate these energies. This seeming starting over is not any kind of loss of momentum. It is the journey itself. Know that the humility and courage to return and be honest means you are on the fast-track home.

I've noticed many people get to this point of their journey and either try to do a U-turn, or they look to find a way to avoid going any further as best they can. At this point, life will certainly already be better than it used to be, even if it is just that we feel a little less stressed and a bit more present. But honestly, there is no way I can convey to you strongly enough that there is so much more life to be had. It seems that fear of meeting the "shadow" stops so many of us from gaining our true inheritance. Our ego tells us that we can't beat this pain or trauma – that this is "just who I am". We need to reach into our real sacred calling and allow the red thread of that to pull us through the fear. The reactive, fearful aspect of ego isn't going to get on our side here. You'll find that it's as tricky as the worst politician who promises you anything and everything but is always seeking to keep power and profit for themselves. Only your heart can cross the divide to find that there was never really any divide. As you'll see and realize in your own time, there is nothing to beat. There is only healing, integration and grace to be met through your increasing congruence with awareness.

It's a truism that all the heavy lifting is at the beginning of any meaningful journey. Just as it is with most things in life, from learning to walk as a child, starting to learn a new language or embarking on a fitness programme, overcoming addictions, and so on, so too, meeting this path of yourself with authenticity and honesty will not be any different. Beginning is so difficult for most of us as we are completely caught in believing that the mind and feeling of false consciousness are who we are. It also seems that almost everything in regular normal society tells us to keep adding to this version of ourselves. In the end, we discover that the way out is not necessarily through as we previously thought, but rather it is the dawning light of awareness that shows you who you really are and what is going on. As you become aware of your light, it moves you to see that you are not the things you have believed in, either consciously or unconsciously, but something much greater.

Not blowing smoke

So, well done for being here, for following the quiet voice inside of you. It means everything to be walking alongside you. Please know that your journey is the whole point of human existence. We've built and discovered so many incredible things in our his-her-stories, but this journey is the most significant movement of life there is. This is why so many great teachers speak of human life as being the "greatest opportunity."

The third dimension of awareness – presence-based awareness

The third dimension of awareness is perhaps the easiest to explain. We are so used to not being it, that we can recognize it in an instant when we touch into it. Quite simply, in the third dimension of awareness you feel like you are actually here in your life, standing on the earth, in this moment. You are of course aware of future and past, but you spontaneously know in your heart of hearts that the present moment is the axis of life, and that this sensation is utterly tangible to you. You cannot believe, or think, or push your way into this. The mind, for all its wonders, cannot create it, but your awareness knows it. The mind and the body actually love this state. You will often hear that meditation involves you quietening your mind, as if that is something you can do. Lots of people hurt themselves with this or simply give up, thinking that meditation is not for them. The way we are talking about is not this. It is not trying to make the mind go quiet or silent or focused; true meditation is the experience of "being" in "presence". Being your being. It is not about satisfying the mind. However, as soon as you do experience the third dimension, which we sometimes simply call presence, you'll find that the mind has gone quieter all by itself, because you are more in your rightful state of existence. Funny that.

Out of time and in time at the same time

In some ways, being in presence is to be outside of time, in that you are living directly from the unfolding isness of this moment. This does not stop day turning to night, the cat needing to be fed, the world going on with its business, and our bodies growing, living, ageing and dying. The interface between the timeless dimension of being and time as we live it more usually, is one of the facets of the great mystery, and it is a place that requires the spontaneous heart of love to understand. There is certainly no way to write or talk about it well, but again, like presence, you already know this "in and out of time at the same time" experience in the depths of yourself.

Some examples of the beauty of the third dimension

What does it mean that you are actually here? Before we jump into a couple of examples, let me just say that most people experience moments of presence every day, but we always pull away into incarnations of life lived in the time lag of future/ past projection because of our conditioning. We also pull into our unhealed pain bodies and trauma, and often out of fear, or sheer bloody-mindedness, because it feels safer as they are feelings we know. If you reflect on any moment where you have really met life through beauty, intimacy, or mortality, you will find the intimate traces and naked beauty of presence there. Please know that at any stage of the journey our practice is not about being at 100 per cent presence, 100 per cent of the time. So many of us get lost struggling to achieve things like this. Rather, please understand that it is more about recognizing those moments of presence when you have them and turning your practice to allowing this incrementally more in all the areas of your life. Meeting as often as we can the quiet place within yourself is the very wholeness and completeness of life that lies under all the pushing and pulling. We only need the tiniest bit of courage and vulnerability to open the areas where we are blocked and reactive. By and by you learn that you can turn to meet them from that deeper place within yourself. Then your life begins to heal and you can walk the path of life more truthfully and authentically. Make this our daily practice and let go of thinking about awakening or "attaining" enlightenment. It is very simple: you are either present, or you are not. Though not being present is also a great teacher once you notice that you are not present. The mind will get dizzy trying to sort this one out, so don't bother. Just come on home, dear human being, to that place where you already are in the here and now.

Relationships and presence

Our intimate relationships and friendships are one of the best places to feel presence or notice our discontinuity. Our connections of family and friendship, with our intimates and even our enemies, are perhaps the biggest mirror in our hall of mirrors. They certainly can be the most entrenched and distorted places, but they offer us the biggest opportunity to know ourselves and to grow.

PAUSE FOR REFLECTION

Take some time to have a journaling session to reflect on your closer relationships:

- Where are your blind spots?
- How do you currently tend to take care of each other?

- Do I listen to others in presence?
- What is your model of love or relating?
- How can you make this more synergistic?

Alone or together

Ordinary human life is the sacred life, and these reflections and questions also apply to ourselves equally when we are alone. Indeed, the relationship with ourselves when we are by ourselves is a great teller of our journey. There is a saying that I'm probably remembering wrongly that goes something like: "You really find out who you are when you are alone with yourself." I'm just going to leave this line hanging here for you to sit with for a little while, and you can let your heart be your guide.

From dependence to connection

If you reflect on your connections and find that they are based on having to be or provide something in order to be accepted, or that we are like this with others, we see that there is a power dynamic or codependence at play. So many of us live this every day that it is taken for normal human life. These dynamics are also reflected in the workplace, our communities, and in every area of daily civil life, and most glaringly on the world's political stage. From the point of view of awakening awareness, it's quite easy to draw the conclusion that "normal" actually is just another word for insane. Allowing presence in our relationships is the exact opposite of these interactions that we are so good at. As you allow your soul and heart into the mix and re-join the family of life, you find that you are more genuinely present with others when you are with them. You are less lost in story, reactions, or trying to be right or to win. Empathy and compassion move more naturally in your heart, and you can just be with them, there is no needing things to be other than they are. This is true too even if the other person is operating from the old model. It only takes one person to make your journey toward the sacredness of life, and that of course, as we said in Chapter 2, is you.

If grace is on your side, you might find that the other person is there with you too. That their presence and yours forms a basis of proper loving care and regard for each other, and when there are slippages, you can both lovingly admit them and support each other in awareness and kindness. You will find that you will move in and out of sync with each other, but as the time-lag begins to evaporate, you can return to yourself and each other more humanly and more quickly. Eventually the comings and goings are simply seen as being part of the flow of awareness. You are just in life with yourself and with each other.

As present awareness deepens you will notice, for example, that when arguments start, you can often see the roots of the problem there and then and bring heart, light and kindness to that place. Instead of wading forward trying to win something that can never be won and that does not actually exist, you realize what is happening and choose not to go into the old reactive patterning. My wife and I have seen our lives utterly transformed for the better individually and as a couple by allowing space for our souls and our humanity with each other in this way. When something comes up it is held in love as soon as possible. Once in awareness, we might need to give each other space for a little while to process and rest with things. We've found that this space only adds to the depth of love and regard that resonates between us. Bringing love and healing between yourself and the other person equally is such a deep opportunity for real growth and healing change when we touch into our fault lines with living awareness. It's quite funny, once you realize – what were at one time your insurmountable difficulties become the greatest opportunities for healing and light. It can almost feel like you're cheating at the game of life, or that you have discovered some great secret.

Presence-based awareness in our relationships means that we have truer beingness with each other, and that we are restored to being family in each other's eyes and hearts. Imagine this way of life as a basis of community, or running our business models, or our systems of governance and foreign policy. Words like "foreign" and "other" would soon fall out of use. If you can imagine this then perhaps it's time we allowed for it and made it so.

False consciousness and the pain-bodied way calls our links with other beings relationships and marriages and so on, but in reality they are business deals based on some kind of attempt at energy exchange. There is often love, because love finds any gap that it can, but we build some high walls unknowingly. We have the underlying hope that one day we'll manage to find the right balance, and if we get it right we'll be queen or king of the mountain and have everything we ever wanted. If only we knew that it takes nothing more than the small inward movement to restore us to sanity and to being family. That the world doesn't have to be on this ever-tightening crash course of limitation and separation. It changes the minute you turn your eyes toward awareness – you set your foot on the path, no matter where you are or what you have done. This leaves us with a question that I've been sitting with my whole life, perhaps you have asked this one too. Why then do we not choose sanity, sacredness, presence and love? Answers on a postcard please.

Meeting your healing

When it comes to our own healing, being present in awareness brings the same rewards as we've just discussed. We can see more clearly what the roots of the unconsciousness or trait are. We can allow ourselves to be a better and more loving friend to ourselves as we seek healing and help. What you will also find now is that any "medicine" you partake of can be more effective because you can make more appropriate choices in the modalities you access, and your kindness and increasingly genuine self-regard allows for change and healing to take place. We can stop holding on so tightly to the old stuff and stories and living in houses made of their brickwork.

If we are caught in the old stories and drama versions of ourselves, healing is much less effective. There will be many slippages back to the old false-consciousness-based self, so we need love and forgiveness and understanding that this is how things are for the longest time. At this stage we allow presence and proactivity, and love and forgiveness will help mediate our recovery and growth. If we are not present, we can't simply be open, there won't be space for change and growth, no matter what our intention is, or what words we say to others. I'm sure you have met people who have tried every modality from meditation to macramé and yet, for all their experiences and attainments, they continue to wear their various pathologies and neuroses like badges of identity. I was certainly that person at times in my life, so I can both empathize and understand that we will never be able to integrate and deal with those things if we won't meet ourselves authentically. Maybe you have even been this person too and that's why you have come here. For me, I never felt like I was actually standing on the earth or that I'd really met another person – I was so cut off in my ideas of who I was. There was always just this voice in my head and these tight feelings that I mistook for myself. I was always trying to do deals with God to get my own way.

Presence recognizes a quieter place that is already within us and is very different to trying to create something. The motion we are talking about is the humble giving up of our somebodiness. It is the end of all that. It will take time, but as you commit to love, this becomes our motivator to move with our journey. Once you taste even a microsecond of freedom, you know that the other way is not any kind of life at all. If we begin to also understand that awareness shines through our hearts and our ordinary human lives, we really begin to be part of life in the way life has always wanted for us. So, to reiterate, the third dimension of awareness is this, it is starting to be here and recognizing presence and proactivity within yourself without trying to add anything to yourself. You start to feel like you are really part of life.

Blockages

We have covered many blocks and dead ends in the paragraphs above. As we've discussed, there is obviously the clinging grasping back to our somebodiness, and there is the imagining we are further on than we are. You'll see a lot of this if you glance at what puts itself forward as the religious or spiritual world in the public realm. With all of this it's almost as if the words courage and ego are sitting in the pans of a balancing scale, and we are both the scales and the holders of the scale.

This is the area that is difficult, that is most likely to be prevalent now, this shifting back and forth between ego identity and the courage to be open, and this goes on for a very long time, so please know there is always more to come. This back and forth is something that everyone has to go through, and it's not really a problem. You are not broken or lost when you slip, though it might feel like it for a while. Meeting this aspect of the path is a very important part of the landscape. It is the curriculum of your own life. As you will be sensing more and more, the old life is so deeply bound into our minds and emotions that when we start to get a glimpse of freedom, it can seem to be too much for us and can trigger all sorts of reactions. Feelings of loss, depression, anxiety, fear and panic can all begin to show up as the generational and self-added things rise up to be met.

The way through

The truth is that these things are showing up to be met, to be healed, and most importantly, integrated or transcended.

They cannot be bypassed, but we do have a choice in how we meet them. If you are moving toward being based more in present awareness, it can seem that this stuff is coming at you quickly and unrelentingly. That is until you drop back to your heart and bring real awareness to what is going on. Then you start to realize that they are showing up because they have not been met properly yet. Even more importantly, if we can begin to welcome these arisings for the gifts that they actually are, we will start to welcome them better when they show up and we can take the opportunity to sit with them, learn the lessons they hold. We free those energies by reintegration and by going beyond concept to bring both awareness into play and taking whatever steps we need to in our human life to help facilitate our growth. I tend to think of this as being the most rock 'n' roll aspect of the whole journey. Rather than bristling to continue the fight with ourselves, we get in there and learn to dance with what needs to be met by us.

The choice that lies before each of us here is whether we will allow understanding of what is going on and to lovingly meet ourselves, or get lost in feeling like all of this is an assault on us, while slipping into blame and shame and attempts at bypassing and so on. Meeting the awareness of the present moment is always the first key. The challenge is to rebel against that voice in us that wants us to lay blame. We can certainly bring understanding to the parts that our parents and society have played in our conditioning, but even with knowing these things, it is us at the end of the day who have to take responsibility for ourselves, for our emotions, our health, and for our journey to healing and wholeness.

If we give ourselves the space and the time we need and we face what forgiveness, love and commitment really mean for us, we will move ahead. We will slip, we will grow, we will slip again. We begin to see that our psychological and spiritual paths are very closely linked, though they are not the same. Awakening is not an arm of personal development or therapy, but without addressing the psychological side of life

and clearing the path to present awareness, we won't have the
space in us to awaken properly. Nor will we have the humanity
and compassion available to us to meet life in the way it asks of
us. If there is an awakening, it will get distorted by the lenses
of what has gone unhealed in us. We have seen this far too
often in teachers and gurus who get lost in money, sex, power
and politics. Let's give up the guru and just be who we are in
presence and heart together.

You might start noticing that grace is playing a bigger
part in your life now. Through grace we learn forgiveness
and love toward ourselves and others, as well as toward our
false consciousness and the traumas and pain body that need
our kindness, presence and healing. Now that real awareness
is becoming part of our lives, we start to reflect and to
understand what it means to give ourselves and others back
into the hands of life or God. All the while with a deepening
knowing that we are taking full responsibility for our lives and
our journey.

Clown shoes

One last tool that we need to see us through, which is so
essential that it cannot be stressed enough, is that we need
to access our good, strong sense of self-deprecating humour,
especially every time our high horse looks down on others, or
we get too grim and entrenched with the stuff we are meeting,
and fortunately kind humour is one of the best gateways to
enter the space of the heart.

The pain body and its nature

The pain body as a concept is very easy to understand, it is
basically the 9/10ths of the iceberg that is under the water and
lies behind the more primal reactive fears in us that tell us that
life is not a gift to us, that we have to trick life in any way we
can in order to get what we need from it. It is the direct result

of being trapped in deep belief that we are not congruent with our souls. This is not to say we should have no fear. The body fears death and damage, we fear the loss of the forms of the people we love, we feel for others and for the mess we've made of the world. Those feelings are part of the real human deal. Without them we have a problem. The pain body is basically our largely unconscious conditioning ossified to such a degree that when active it tries to suck everything into its field to react either outwardly or inwardly with terrible force to prove its own existence.

We have long known about the pain body. Carl Jung referred to it as the shadow. The Buddha referred to it by the term *samskaras* or negative tendencies. The oldest and most accurate word for it, and the one we will switch to now for the rest of the book, is *vasana*, which means "a deeply worn groove into which everything flows". The term *samskaras* captures the reactivity of what we are talking about, in that the tendencies move into a whirlpool of thought-forms and then into action but misses out the root or the source of where those thought forms come from. This is dangerous as it makes us think that we can override things by thinking new thoughts. You often see people trapped in this loop for years, trying to replace their thoughts so that they might feel whole and healed. So we will stick with *vasana*, and understand that the other iterations can help us conceptually. But this work is so important it is often the difference between life and death, so we will throw semantics aside and get to the heart of it. We can leave the arguing about terms to those who find value in that avoidance.

Every person has *vasana* in the background, because we have learned the mistake of separateness as being who we are, rather than our uniqueness grounded in the wholeness of reality and what is. Thankfully for most people it is not usually active unless under great duress or in certain situations where it takes over their person. However, without really knowing it, these grooves do form a majority of our mind and experience in everyday life. Our sense of separateness or duality is affirmed continuously, even throughout the most normal day. We fail to see the gift of life that we are, that other people are, that the planet is. We reduce things and each other to only having material value and can't learn that even the most difficult things in life are trying to show us the road home.

We tend see the reactive forms of *vasana* arise around certain things on a personal level, like family visits for example, where we are fine one minute and explode in rage almost for no reason the next. If we are lucky, it can be quite comedic, think Basil Fawlty spiralling off from some tiny thing into a huge explosion. We usually try our best to learn to live with it as a largely unregistered phenomena, humiliating as it is when it happens to us. However, in some people it is much more active, and dangerous, often deadly. I'm sure you have come across people who seem infused with a simmering level of threat, or physical/psychological violence around them like bad air. It can also be truly explosive or sharp, and I'm sure you have seen this too. Think road rage, racism, rape, malignant narcissism, emotional manipulation, codependent pushing and pulling and physical abuse, going out looking for fights, gang violence and murder. It is in both men and women and it doesn't favour or spare one over the other, no matter what we might pretend, but it manifests all the above in us with its particular flavours depending on our modes of being.

Unmet *vasana* is one of the reasons why so few of us are actually present in life; we are overwhelmed by separation, and not even our beliefs and tribes will glue us back together. Those things always end up as us versus them, and only truth and love can help us with this. *Vasana* lies behind all the projections we live through, the masks, defences, lies, and the shows we put on. It is the root of insecurity; the thing that keeps us separate from all that we really want in life that has meaning. It is why we stay so attached to things which don't serve us well, trying to make them make do. Perhaps think of *vasana* this way: if false consciousness is the mind of delusion, then *vasana* is the unhealthy bowels of it. This is why your healing is so entwined with your sacred path. Stepping forward lovingly allows so much of what is delusory to begin to be transcended. Even things that have been held as our most cherished beliefs will start to go if they are not real. The ego and the body of *vasana* are going to fear this process, but walk forward with love and courage, dear one. What you are left with on this journey is yourself as truth and as the gift of your sacredness and ordinariness. As you integrate *vasana* you will start to find that you feel freer in your life, perhaps in small ways at first but they are deeply tangible.

Inward

While it's easy to focus on *vasana* that moves outwardly in violence and so on, especially in the past few hundred years, it is equally important to discuss with you how it can also turn inward and be implosive. When it is inwardly turned, it is the core condition that leads to self-harm, suicide, some forms of schizophrenia, depression, anxiety, codependence, narcissism, addiction and so many other disorders. There are of course biological dis-eases that underlie things like depression and schizophrenia, but for most people all these things come some way within the scope of *vasana* – so they can be addressed and healed more easily than we can possibly imagine if the will and honesty of awareness is there. This is why the spontaneous nature of the third dimension of awareness – present awareness – is so vital. It's amazing that this elephant in the room is so little talked about. Thankfully there are some psychologists and doctors starting to see things more wholly now, but they are still quite rare. Meeting this aspect of *vasana* would be of such benefit to both sufferer and society if this were to be understood and brought into the open more, which is why on this path it falls to each of us to actively participate in our own healing. Meeting this and learning your healing makes for true heroism. We think of soldiers as heroes, but the one who turns to face themselves, that is the greater one. This is courage of the highest order. There should be a medal, and kings and queens should bow before you. I mean this with all my heart, and if they won't or can't – I will. Here's to those who have the courage of vulnerability, awareness and love.

Manipulation

Something we don't realize is that unhealed *vasana* makes us truly susceptible to manipulation by cults, codependent partners and friends, as well as the political, the divisive, the power hungry and the greedy. Basically, anyone who wants to take our time, energy, sexuality, life-force, money, space, and so on. The news media, politics, as well as film, advertising, gaming and musical industries have all learned how to use our *vasana* for their gain. Even the field of spirituality, yoga and wellbeing often use these fracture lines and grooves to catch us. There are entire branches of sciences dedicated to the support of keeping us held for no other reason than to capitalize on us in the worst sense of that word through the exploitation of *vasana*. There is a reason for the phrase "Sex sells". So does fear, anger, entitlement and promises of a better life through consumption and duality. Sadly, others can see our traits so easily, but we rarely see them for ourselves. If we want to have any freedom in this life, we have to look into the guts of things, at the depths of the iceberg, it is this serious. But as ever I ask you not to take my word for any of this. If you are making this journey, you have to look for yourself, understand for yourself and decide on your next step for yourself. Of course, that can be with a teacher or guide to help you, but if you are not questioning and bringing awareness for yourself, you are not making this journey, it's something else. But once you dare to look, suddenly the word rebellion looks very real. Because if you do look, if you dare heal, you are going to be breaking all the apparent rules.

By extension, we can easily see now how *vasana* has communal, national and global incarnations. It begins in the personal but scales up globally very quickly, and of course these traits have built and earned compound interest over the centuries. It is the root of war and fascism, racism, rape, empire creation, religious persecution and colonialism. It is why we feel the need to create borders and walls, it is the breath behind the words "mine" and "ours" and "others". It is at the heart of insane versions of capitalism and hoarding and not contributing to life. Look at any country with the eyes of awareness and you can quickly see the particular flavour of *vasana* at play there. They look like different expressions, but they all have the same heart.

PAUSE FOR REFLECTION

As a reflective exercise pick any country that comes to mind. The USA, UK, Israel, India, France, Germany, the Congo, wherever. Allow yourself to settle in presence-based awareness and with non-reactivity as best you can. Perhaps even look with empathy and kindness. Simply ask yourself what tendencies you can see that are bearing fruit in that country right now. What grooves can you see that things keep flowing back to, no matter what? Grab your pen and journal if you like and note them. The things you will see are things that we are never allowed to talk about. I invite you to notice the culture and threat of silence around so many of them. That quiet – and also sometimes quite vocal and physical – sense of threat and violence is one of the ways we can recognize *vasana* very easily, it is how it continues to have its hold. It often feels like living with an unpredictable abusive partner, and this is usually mirrored in our choices of leadership in the present day.

Our dear selves

The exercise above is quite easy to do. When it comes to looking at ourselves things get much more opaque. But please hear me, there is no pressure to try to jump into this and get it sorted all at once. It is just important to lay this subject out as clearly as we can here. How and when you meet this, if at all, is entirely up to you. In fact, I want to remind you that if you see any of this stuff in yourself, go as carefully and lovingly as you can, and allow yourself to get therapeutic or spiritual help if needed. A good Jungian therapist or a body psychotherapist are wonderful helpers to have on board if you can access them, as well as leaning into your own resources like taking time in nature, *arya mouna*, physical routines and so on. Just as we discussed in the sections on false consciousness and the support of using novel experiences, these tools are vital here for balance and staying open.

Indicators

Vasana has some clear and unmissable indicators. Here we will look at a few of them to help you see how things work more clearly. In the sections following this discussion, we will look at how we might begin to meet *vasana* in our own lives and in the world around us. I think you already know what the keys are to help heal and reintegrate your own aspects of this within yourself.

The following short list might help you start to see that you can begin working with what you need to. It's beyond important to understand that without honestly meeting this side of the work, any awakening or advancement we believe we've made will in time only collapse in on itself, the consequences of which can be very difficult for yourself and for others.

A closed fist/intensity

One of the most noticeable traits of *vasana* is that it carries an intense charge. It takes over the person experiencing it when it is active, and this can be sustained like rage, or it might almost operate quite unconsciously but will flash through the individual if they go near one of their triggers. We could cite innumerable examples of this, for example try telling someone who is infected with racism that they are being racist; an alcoholic that they have a problem; or try pointing out systemic injustices that have been incorporated into the frameworks of our societies and dare to question their continuance. These are quite gross examples, but you can see the flame ignite almost instantly in so many cases and the actions that will flow toward you if you do question things.

Vasana always has a squeezing and cutting-off quality in both its outward and inner forms. The person may be exploding at you in rage or withdrawn in a state like there is a bell jar covering them, but they are cut off from sense, communication and love, anything you say to them will be twisted to fit the *vasana*'s narrative. When it's ourselves, it is these factors of not hearing, of being lost in raging thoughts, egoic defensiveness, the inclination to attack, or to disappear into numbness, that show us we're in a *vasana* episode. This is what we have to look out for.

Seeking continuance

Vasana always seeks to continue the pain, whether that is by pushing within the person themselves or looking to attack or trigger another. Have you ever had that thing where you are so desperate for an argument that you poke and poke at someone to try to get them to lash back, then you say: "Look, see, I told you that you were like this …" It also seeks continuance physically – it wants a fight or it wants to press down and micromanage and control the lives of ourselves or another. It's important to recognize that *vasana* generates such reactivity in this way and tries to pass pain into you because that is far easier than admitting we don't know what is right or real or best for us. Yet admitting we have a problem is the only way to begin any healing.

A sense of righteousness or exceptionalism

If a person, group or country is always going on about how right they are, or that they are the best, or that they have to argue, or push and pull and manipulate, making fights and wars to show their rightness or their exceptionalism, you know that there is *vasana* beneath this. It often displays as narcissism of course, because it is that in many ways. *Vasana* and narcissism are interlinked, so are codependency and addiction. The addiction to being right by any means, whether that is through high-status egoic proclamations, or by being the lowest of the low, you know the kind of talk: "I am the worst, I told you I was not good enough," "No one will ever love me." Whichever way *vasana* expresses in us, it's always that kind of keeping the attention and focus on ourselves by any means, always ego proving that ego is right, that make *vasana* so obvious.

Creating duality and distraction

Closely linked to the above examples, we also find that *vasana* seeks to create or widen dualistic situations in order to exploit them. "If you are not with us, you are against us." Or: "They are all against me." Forcing dualism into a situation is often done to get some of that false power that passes as the capital and currency in the normal world, but it also keeps us from looking at the perpetrators and the causes of these distractions. It keeps us from ever moving forward. *Vasana* is the ultimate personification of filibustering and we can see so many examples of this in the business of the world, but it's also in each of us at some level and will be acting through unconsciously unless we choose awareness and healing.

Spreading around and spiritual bypassing

As we discussed, *vasana* is thankfully not active a lot of the time in the majority of people, but the world at this time is really doing its best to spread it around to capitalize on it through quite simple and gross longstanding mechanisms, so it is becoming much more of a daily reality in many low-level or unconscious ways. It then perpetuates its divisive nature, either explosively or quietly, with greater and greater regularity.

In many ways, we might say that are living in the century of *vasana*, just as we can look at the 20th century and see that it was the century of holocaust – we can also see that the pain of then has led directly into this century through the lack of awareness and healing around our collective pasts.

We really have to take every opportunity to use our lives and these times to move more into awareness and conscious action, not just for our own good, but for the very survival of the planet and all the life here. We don't need to go chasing down our *vasana*, that way leads to a lot of poorliness, but we do need to commit to ourselves that when it does arise, or that when we can see that someone is trying to trigger that in us, we will meet it with awareness and love and not just do that thing of trying to pretend that it's not there. If we commit to meeting it as soon as we notice its movement in us, it honestly doesn't have to be so much of a problem.

But if we carry on pretending, if we keep up the charade that we are something other than we are – and many spiritual people and teachers do this as they want to be seen as being whole and holy – then we just make a whole bunch of pain for ourselves and the world around us. Why should we be so ashamed and full of pretending? That's part of the mechanism of *vasana* and its desire for continuance. We don't need to tell anyone that we are engaged in our deep healing. It is far better to do the work with honesty and authenticity without drawing many others into our process. Too many of us try to avoid our own shadow, and many people get into spirituality or religion to try to cover up this area in the hope that they won't have to deal with it. Perhaps they are convinced that there is a magic bullet hidden somewhere that will just take all the pain somehow. Spirituality without shadow work or healing is craziness and is at best performative and optical in its nature. This is truly the heart of spiritual bypassing. It has been rampant in religions and spiritual circles forever, but what is amazing is that bypassing too, when noticed, is an indicator we can depend on to show us what is really going on, and then it can help to take us homeward.

Approaching healing

The simple invitation here is to turn with honest integrity toward integration and healing by first admitting that there is a problem and that we don't know what to do about it. Once you know where you are, you can actually start to see what is available to you. The key to this step is not to expect any great miracle, but to simply take the smallest real step you can each day. These small steps might just be the most important things we can do to save ourselves and the world.

When you heal *vasana* through integration, you not only get all of your life energy back that has been trapped for so long under the armouring and the fear, but you also get the benefits of healing your life – you get yourself back. That drop of pain, of fear and reactivity that we've fed for so long, gives up its hidden treasure of life energy – the *vasana* is removed from the world to be replaced by love and reality. The world literally is a better place for each increment of your returning to wholeness. You no longer contribute to the negative energy field of personal, communal and global *vasana*, and this has a huge effect in innumerable ways. The same is true when your awakening begins to dawn, the ripples around you and in the lives of others are unmeasurable. Your awakening is not just a personal thing, it sets the world right, natural and congruent with reality by the degree of you.

Beginning to heal your *vasana* will turn you into what Jungians tend to call a "transitional person", as I mentioned before. This means that by daring to address your healing and what it means to be truly human, you are often going against the unspoken rules of family, tribe, culture or country – these things usually seek to continue their particular feeding of their secrets and grooves.

Notice the areas where we have to walk on eggshells. Notice what is "allowed" or "not allowed". This is a time when boundaries and self-care are essential. I would ask you to take some time to reflect in your journal about the resources you have at this point and are prepared to bring in. Healing is a process of awareness and integration. The reason I waited until this part of the book to talk about *vasana* is that we have already started working with many of the tools you might need. Working with novel experiences, embodiment, deepening into awareness, developing your daily meditation practice and so on.

The most important tool of course is your awareness. The moment you spot active *vasana* in yourself, simply move to awareness as quickly as you can and give yourself space. It will seek to keep on going, so space while meeting it with love is really important. Perhaps take yourself out for a couple of hours, walk or take yourself away for a while on retreat. It takes practice to allow awareness and a loving hands-on approach, but they are the great keys. As you learn your *vasana* and the things that trigger it into flame, you might see that you need some outside help, and please with my hand on my heart, hear me – getting help around addictions, codependencies, old family wounds, allowing for therapies like acupuncture, massage, body work and so on are really ways of taking care of, and using your resources to support yourself. They are not ends in themselves, and the therapist might not understand the sacred angle that you are coming from, but allow yourself what you need. Imagine if we spent the money we spend on streaming television, and take-outs, on healing foods, massage, colonics and appropriate therapies instead. We will look at aligning our resources a bit further on, but you get what I'm saying, I'm sure.

The way through

In closing out this chapter, I would like to quickly share with you six tools that I have used on my own journey and that I have seen help my own students. After this quick look at these, I'll share with you a beautiful integrative meditation that is really helpful at this juncture of our travels.

Let's look at each of these tools very briefly; every one of them is worthy of a book in its own right, and so we're not seeking to go into these here in any great depth, but it's worth looking in order to introduce you to a range of steps or tools you might care to access for yourself.

1. Admittance and responsibility
Admitting to ourselves that there's a problem and taking responsibility is perhaps the greatest tool in the box we have. Without this step, there is no next step. The opposite of it is denial, bypassing, the blaming of others and continued *vasana* in ourselves. Though other people may have been involved in the things that have happened to us, this stage is ultimately where we understand that the way forward is to take responsibility with ourselves, including the stuff of others that we carry that we are not responsible for. This doesn't mean entering into stories of shame and blame, it means entering the courageous path of love. This taking of responsibility is necessary both in terms of psychological healing, and for having room to hear your soul and deepening into it. It does not mean we know any answers as to how to proceed, but it means that we are willing to stand and say: "Okay then, let's see what's real here." I promise you, as hard as this might seem to be, and for most of us this is a really tough step at first, at some point you will look back down the path and see how far you have come, and you will be indescribably grateful for the moments where you have made this choice.

2. Asking for reflection from those you trust
This one needs a lot of care, but if your relationships and friendships are moving with consciousness you can have an agreement to kindly point out to each other when things are out of harmony. Then allowing each other to be a heartful and

helpful support as you process things. Great care is needed as we can easily slip into blaming or one-upmanship. Yet, with a good dose of love and humour, our relationships, by their very nature of being a major crucible for our experience, can also be incredibly supportive of our journey. Not that we are each other's therapists, or projects for repair. The kind of loving support we are talking about would really form a wonderful aspect to what we might call a conscious relationship.

3. Self-care

We hear so much about self-care these days, but as part of a personal programme of genuine positive self-regard as we address our *vasana,* it moves from being a nice idea to being a fundamental expression and communication with ourselves. Self-care in this light centres on balancing our nature mentally, emotionally, physically and spiritually. There are so many caring modalities you might want to reach into.

I have found the following to be really effective and helpful:

- Aryuvedic cooking and medicines
- Learning about boundaries
- Journaling
- Yoga – eight limbs
- *Qiqong* and acupuncture
- Massage
- Myofascial release
- Body psychotherapy

As you proceed and allow greater self-care, you might decide to try any or all of these and more. Again, we are not doing these things to try to escape or bypass what we need to meet, but having ways to process and balance things through tried and tested means such as these is fundamental.

4. Inner-child work

Inner-child work is where we work by ourselves or with a practitioner to access the life energies in ourselves that have been trapped or cut off for a long time. Carl Jung noted that this often takes place at the stage where we begin to lose our innocence, around age six or seven; it can be earlier if there has been trauma, and of course it can also occur at other stages in life or be compounded as we get older. So, you might be working with your inner teen, your inner 30-something, or your inner 60-year-old. It depends at what age the conditioning or break took hold.

Generally, though, the inner child is a returning to the point of the loss or break, not building stories about what happened, though that can be helpful to recognize at first. Then we move through our process to freedom and the return of life energy. It is more about re-bonding with those aspects of our lost selves and actually being there for our inner child, instead of trying to push things away so as to be someone our *vasana* or false consciousness imagines is the person we are meant to be. It is the most beautiful act of self-discovery, and, while ultimately symbolic in many ways, far from being childish, or making us naïve, we regain our innocence, but with the wisdom of life experience added to the mix.

If you are feeling like your life is going nowhere or just don't have much joy or spontaneity in you, this might be a good place to look. Spiritually working with the inner child gives us a much deeper access to our own soul and the expression of who we really are.

5. Reorganizing your resources

As we discussed a little earlier, we now find ourselves with more choices in how we proceed. One thing that can be a real sticking point for people is our relationship to money. Spirituality and yoga have become part of the wellbeing industry in a lot of the world, and while we are talking about many different healing modalities in this chapter, it is really important to underline that what we are talking about is not buying into a lifestyle or anything that is for sale. The path of awareness is for everyone – the commercial aspect that touches everything in our world does not need to be feared or swallowed wholesale. Your healing and awakening have got nothing to do with money. We cannot buy a stairway to heaven, but if you find any of the offerings helpful from those worlds because they help you build your health, for example, or process difficult old stuff, then do consider availing yourself of them to meet your needs.

One thing I found radically helpful was to allow myself to organize my resources around my journey. For instance, getting help where I needed it, such as acupuncture to balance my physical health and energies after a very profound illness. I've also found that engaging with travel in a non-tourist way to explore some of the aspects of my human life has been tremendously helpful. I also bought a lot of books, attended retreats and yoga courses and so on. Not looking for completion in them, but just looking to see what was real within each thing I felt drawn to and leaving the rest. In the end, of course, it's just us and our journey, but very often our finances and resources dribble away in all sorts of directions in life quite unconsciously and take our energy with them. I changed my insurances, paid off my mortgage, cancelled all TV and app subscriptions except those directly for work, and the difference was amazing. This allowed me to engage with healing, therapies, classes and self-care so much more. You are free to do as you like of course around your money and every aspect of your life, but this is just a thought I wanted to run by you, as I found it made life so much better to allow this focus around resources.

6. *Shenpa* practice and beingness-based meditation
In a few moments we'll try a version of a type of meditation called *shenpa* practice. First, to give you a little background to it, *shenpa* meditation is an old Tibetan way of working

that arose to help the practitioner be able to meet and process emotions as they arise. *Shenpa* means "things that are arising". It is a deeply helpful and transformative practice that goes very well with all that we have been talking about and is wonderful to pair with inner-child work.

The practice we are about to do takes a heart-centred and beingness-based approach, so that you can benefit most fully and have self-compassion more available to you. This is essential through the whole *vasana* journey. It has been found in study after study that beingness-based practices, where you are establish a good physical sense of presence are the safest types of meditations – they are not known to cause any triggering or trauma reawakening. Connecting into the body and gently meeting what is there and bringing acknowledgement and kindness to it is so important. There is no rush. Please be gentle and persistent, one baby step at a time.

Meditation – the practice of your three hearts – *shenpa* version

Gently gift these words to yourself as you take a comfortable sitting position. Please allow around 20 minutes for your practice once or twice daily.

As we did with the previous meditation, allow yourself to be at ease and simply become aware of yourself sitting within the room or space that you are in. Allow yourself to notice your natural breathing, and how breath moves your body. Don't take over your breathing or focus on it particularly, just feel your body moving with life and breath.

Allow awareness of your feet, legs and lower body.

Allow awareness of your spine, relaxing your back, your shoulders, arms and hands.

Allow awareness of your neck and head. Your face softening.
You can close your eyes if you like or keep them open and easy.

Allow awareness of your chest and heart.
Take a moment to notice you can feel the subtle movement of
breath at the level of your heart too.

Allow awareness of your abdomen.

Allow awareness of your groin, and your reproductive and
excretory organs.
Feel that your whole body is welcome here.
If you feel dis-ease or criticism toward your body, allow yourself
to meet that kindly rather than trying to push it away.
Can you allow a little love to go to that place?

Awareness of your body.
Awareness of the space around you without naming, reacting or
labelling things.

Awareness of how your body simply feels right now.

Allowing yourself to drop more and more into this growing
clarity that is already within you.

Letting go of any idea of having a meditation experience or
getting it right.
Just meeting this moment, with kindness in your abdomen and
heart, and the sense of the life in your body.

Noticing the gentle movement at the level of your physical
heart.
Enjoying feeling into the physical nature of your heart.
The rhythm. The spaces within the chambers. The space
around your heart.

Take a couple of minutes here and feel grounded in your whole body and meeting your physical heart.

Now you have become aware of the emotional dimension of your heart.
Allowing for any vulnerability to simply be there as you settle into your emotional heart.

Feeling the energy of your emotional heart, notice that you can feel the spaces between the movements of emotion. We might call this heart of emotion and the space our second heart.
Please take a few moments here and continue allowing ease to open up within you as you settle into the experience of energy and space.

Awareness of the space that your mind is taking place in, the movements, spaces, and attachments of thoughts. Not trying to change them, but just noticing from your deepening awareness.

Awareness of the space that your emotional heart is taking place in, the movements of feelings, the spaces, and attachments. Not trying to change anything, but just noticing from awareness.

Awareness of the room you are in, the feeling of your whole body, your breath, your mind.
Witnessing your physical heart and your emotional heart.

You may notice that your awareness is aware of a stillness in or behind your heart.
A still point or a sense of living dynamic silence.
Relaxing into greater ease.
Allowing yourself without grasping toward it to know this is the centre of yourself.
We might call this deeper space the spiritual heart. In Sanskrit this is called atman.

Take a few minutes and be in the experience of your sacred heart.

Awareness of the room you are in.

Awareness of your body, breath, mind, feelings, senses, and your three hearts within the sense of simple beautiful nowness.

Without disturbing yourself, notice if anything is arising for you in this moment.
Notice if there is anything you are stuck with, if there is pain in mind or emotion, if there is unconsciousness or reactivity or vasana *moving.*

Not trying to get rid of it, but instead noticing where you feel this in your body and say "Hello" to it.
"Hello."

You can say gently to yourself: "I am here for you."

"Don't be afraid."

"I will not abandon you."

"I love you."

Let go in this moment of trying to let go.
You might ask: "What is it you need me to know?"

Don't look for answers in your mind but allow the statements and questions to simply exist within you.
You may feel something shift in your felt sense later, or an answer come to you in guidance.

If something is very tight or painful, you may wish to put one hand on your heart.

And you can drop into this space the word "soften".

"Soften."

"Soften."

After a few moments allow yourself to drop all efforts, all questions and words and to rest in the wholeness, beauty and dignity of the ground of being. Simply being. Notice your own experience for yourself.

Continue sitting for as long as you wish.

... and when you are ready, be aware of the feeling of life in your body, the space of the room around you, your senses and your breath.
The quality of light in the room.

When you are ready bring your practice to a close with a sense of gratitude of having turned up for yourself.
And so, this meditation ends.

SIGNPOST 6

MOVING FROM FEAR TO LOVE

In many ways, a lot of what follows now is a consolidation of everything that has gone before us on our journey. While we have tried to be very clear in all that we have spoken about so far, it is important to remind ourselves that nothing here is just for the sake of being information. The words and how they are conveyed may or may not suit you, but everything here is only really a pointer to encourage you to allow for a deeper embracing of your humanity and, therefore, your healing and awakening.

To reiterate from the introduction, at no point do I go along with the idea that you awaken and all of your troubles disappear. Awakening and healing are continuous. There is no end to them. We talked about spiritual bypassing in the previous chapter, and I wanted to state again very clearly where I stand on this. I know I'm rather breaking the fourth wall here, but this is not a play or a movie. It's just you and me. I have no wish to get you to see things my way or call me guru or teacher or any of those things. The teacher is in you, and the teacher is the life you have right now. You are not a puzzle to be solved and your life has value. Otherwise, you simply would not have it. As realization takes hold, it will change how you see your life situations, and soul awareness (presence) is central to this, but it is not all that you are, and your life is not disposable. Which is something you might get to thinking if you've read certain types of spiritual books. I'm sure many will argue for this position, and if you encounter this argument as I often do, just let them have it. Their life is their life, and you are here and now.

I draw this distinction out again because Signpost 6 is really about starting to see our humanness with love. There is a lot less effort involved, though we might need reminding every now and then. But generally, because your awareness sees beyond false consciousness more often, and because you are learning what it means to work with your particular *vasana*s, love starts to arise and respond much more freely in your heart and actions toward yourself and others. Before this, perhaps, love was there, but there may have been an overlay of fear or a pulling back from being in life. Things may have also manifested as pity or a sort of numbness. Or there may have been a stepping forward to meet situations with a bit more ego, perhaps to look like somebody spiritual, or a good person, our old identity trap. But the twofold signifier here is that fear, numbness, and somebodiness begin to decrease, and you start living and responding with a more spontaneous loving basis within yourself. This also begins to show as compassion more often when it meets suffering in others.

PAUSE FOR REFLECTION

Look out for tangible signs of this shift and perhaps journal about your observations, fears, reservations, and your questions. Are you aware of the source of these things in you? How are you meeting yourself with greater love and proactivity?

Take some time to reflect on your sense of "oneness" or a "wholeness" to the underlying nature of life in people, beings and the natural world around you.

Blockages

There are three main blockages to look out for at this stage:

Jumping to the end and ego

Once real present awareness begins to establish, the blockages within really begin to decrease to be replaced by a sense of being able to meet and process things more and more. However, we can only meet things as they arise, and as much as our ego might want or try to skip the journey, we cannot simply jump to the end, as if there were an end. You will often come across people and teachers who claim to be "fully cooked", but the very claim itself shows that it is simply not true. While we live a human life, we will have all that goes along with humanity operating within us, the only difference is awareness.

Though things are consolidating for us now and we are becoming more congruent with awareness, we will still from time to time get caught by our more egoic-based identity attaching itself to any progress we make. Ego is not our enemy, it tries to make us feel complete through what it knows, but then it tends to hold us back within its sphere of limited knowing. It's easy to spot, we will think we've got it now and we know what we are doing and the outcomes are guaranteed. If we are hearing that voice, it's time to drop back a bit.

Fears of friends and family

As you will be re-evaluating so many aspects of life by centring more into awareness, you will obviously seem quite different to the old you in regard to your energies and tastes. Your friends and family are going to worry about you changing. It may be that you have changed, and their tendency is to do all they can to keep on being exactly the same. They may still treat you as the person you used to be, and perhaps something in you wants to show them how much you have changed. You probably want to share the good news of your discoveries with them, which leads to a merry dance indeed. We can, if we are not careful, think we know better than our friends and family. That old ego loves this stuff.

Wanting to save everyone

We might also think that now we are getting straight, that we suddenly have to try to start saving everyone. This is perfectly understandable, but question yourself if this is showing up. Where is that desire coming from in you? It takes a long time for consciousness to settle once things start to move and there is more getting straight to do than can ever be conveyed. "Getting straight" is a good metaphor for starting to come out of the almost hallucinatory state of immersion in the dualistic nature that we lived in for so long, and of course we want to help other people. I'm not saying don't help, I'm saying go slow. Be grounded, be real, or we just create more mess.

The way through

I think we're possibly getting into broken-record territory now, but as usual it's really all about patience, love and attending with heart and awareness, all the way. We might describe this as an open-handed quality of being. If you will reflect back on how not being in awareness feels, how false consciousness and *vasana* feels, we might say that they have a fist-like quality, a tightness or gripping sensation to them. As we move forward it's almost as if we are starting to meet life with a more open hand. More open-handed toward ourselves and toward those closer to us. You will probably find that you also feel this openness toward people more generally around you in the world. Though this might come and go for a while.

You will find that you become more open to allowing experience, allowing your feelings, allowing yourself time to process. In regard to others, you will find that fear has started to turn to acceptance, and you can allow others to be who they are without wanting them to be a certain way. The most important thing here is to continue allowing your practice to deepen, to keep on allowing the adventure of growing awareness, to keep on allowing the mystery of the quiet place within you that comes before mind and emotion and even sensation. Allowing does not create it, but it lets us experience the truth of ourselves. We can practice this allowing throughout the day.

Here's a practice for you

When you next visit a relative or a friend who you generally find a bit difficult, see how it is to allow yourself not to react back. Can you instead lean in to be an open hand of awareness and presence? Can you allow yourself not to say the thing you always say to them or make the face you often make? As you sit with them, allow yourself to see past the surfaces to the place that comes first in them, even if they have no idea that they are so much more.

This way of being with others is such a great inner teacher from the frontline of your ordinary experience. The not surprising big news is you'll fail and fail and fail, and yet what we perceive as failures are nothing of the sort. As long as awareness and love lie behind our attempts to turn up, there is wisdom to be gained. There is no such thing as getting it right as a human being, but we can be present. Soul meeting soul in awareness, regardless of our seemingly different outer situations. This is such a gorgeous practice which you might find becomes a large part of your daily reality because, well, people.

Love enough to accept change and growth

We find that the increasing movement from fear to love allows us to start meeting change and growth in a much more ready way. Before (and still, perhaps) there might have been a voice in your head trying to get you to be a somebody, but as long as you keep coming back to loving heart-centred awareness, you'll be alright. Real love is needed at every step of the way because you are not going to end up as the person you think you are going to end up as. Awareness and awakening are a whole different order of being, unlike anything that we can come up with in our minds or that our egos can project ahead of ourselves. Amazingly though, when you do know yourself more in this way, you'll realize that you have always been yourself. The ways we have been living might cause us some sorrow for a while when we realize what fools we have been. This too needs our profound forgiveness.

Surrender, soothe, forgive

A little formula that you can carry in your pocket from here on out is "surrender, soothe, forgive". Which is really what you've been learning to allow up to this point. Surrendering your ego to enter into this moment. Soothing and dropping past the energies of the conditioning and reactivity that you've been carrying, and so entering into presence – the key to the act of forgiveness itself. Three words with more power than atom bombs.

Some words on trauma

I just want to say to you that if you have come to practice or meditation to help you deal with past or present trauma then my heart really goes out to you. Trauma is one of the most difficult things we have to deal with as human beings, and connecting with spiritual practice is a really helpful way to approach a path of healing. In this short section I want to look at some approaches that I have found to be effective and helpful when combined with the type of practices we are sharing here, but I also want to gently draw your attention to a few traps we sometimes can fall into, which just might save you from some difficult cul-de-sacs.

There are a number of amazing people who have researched

trauma and healing in far greater depth than we can go into
in this volume, so for further details see the recommended
reading list at the end of this book. But I just want to say
to you with all the love in the world, in my experience as a
teacher and a fellow sufferer, that I've found that only an
embodied and loving approach will serve us well here. Trauma
creates its own kind of *vasana*, its own kind of grooves. We
might say that it is holographic in nature in that even the
smallest aspect of it contains the whole picture, which means
that trauma's presence and effects often lie far outside of
our direct consciousness but can fire up and into its fullness,
seemingly without reason.

Trauma can come from a whole range of experience:
violence, abandonment, betrayal, racial abuse, sexual abuse,
systemic injustice, community belief systems, codependency,
war, post-traumatic stress disorder (PTSD), inequality and so
much more. I know you know how long this list could be. All
that we have talked about up to this point can be really helpful
in helping us see the wood for the trees – learning about your
awareness, going beyond false consciousness and projection,
allowing change to help you move, learning about reactivity
and choosing to respond, understanding *vasana* and deepening
into present awareness, and perhaps most importantly getting
a sense of your soul at the heart of it all. And of course, our
little formula of "surrender, soothe, forgive".

The big forgive here, of course, is to forgive ourselves for
having trauma, forgive ourselves for all the ways we have acted
out and tried to create safety, even if that was from blinding
ego and rage. That part of you has got you here, and you are
alive because of it. We have to allow gratitude for all that we
have done to survive. The only question now is, can we allow
ourselves to begin to move to a better healing with awareness
and soul playing a more congruent part in our lives?

One way that the teachings here differ greatly from a lot
of the canon of spiritual guidance is that I am in no way ever
going to suggest to you that all you have to do is stay present,

or awaken, or keep mindful, or that once you know the true nature of reality you'll have no problems any more. I've been practising for around 45 years at this time, and teaching for 35 years and I have never once met anyone who has overcome the effects of trauma through spiritual practice purely on its own. It surely helps when met with sincerity, and will help you understand things with greater insight, but it doesn't make things vanish. I feel it is important to watch out for the type of teachings that place things out of reach in that "just stay mindful or present" sort of way that we hear a lot of now. It is actually a terrible way to keep you hooked into an ecosystem that is usually serving its own purposes rather than helping you toward loving awareness. This type of thing is easy to spot if you find yourself feeling that no matter what you do, you'll never be quite enough somehow. Whereas the path of realization reveals to the practitioner that you are loved from within, regardless of who we have been, or what we may or may not have done. Not by the teacher, mind you, but by the "what is" – God, if you will.

As you have seen, and are hopefully discovering for yourself, it is not that hard to begin to move beyond false consciousness, and with trauma this shift helps us to see straight and enter into a more loving relationship with ourselves. A sincere meditation practice that offers a method to lead you into consciousness and embodiment can also help so much with that shift. But meditation is not always right for people, as trauma flashes can trigger very easily when things inevitably come up, or if we are trying to control our breath and so on. We need to bring things into the light very gently, and less direct approaches such as conscious walks in nature, *arya mouna* and gentle yoga practices that include reflective aspects like the *yamas* and *niyamas* can be helpful. Remember also to use positive novel experiences to help you gently open things up and create inner space. Meditation is not a panacea and may not be right for your spiritual or healing path. Often looking after yourself through diet and a daily walk in the woods will be far more helpful than meditation. Once things are steadier then maybe we can look at meditation, but there is no rush. If you are suffering from trauma that has moved to have schizophrenic elements, I would say just don't meditate or do yoga nidra at all, stick to physical novel ways of working that include creativity, movement and art, for example. It is better to be safe, very gradual, integrative and real, than ever to push at all.

If you suffer from, or are in a situation where trauma is currently ongoing, it is not going to change by staying present. Spirituality can be a bit like going up onto a high roof so you can see what the layout of the land is and this is really useful, but the thing is that you can't live on the roof, which is what "just stay present" or "just stay mindful" or "you are not your body" might seem to be saying sometimes. Change only comes when we occupy and live in the building, and also take what we learn onto the streets with us. A better way to approach spirituality, not just regarding trauma but overall, is to realize that while being on the roof and having a wider view is lovely, it takes embodiment and living with awareness daily to turn things to practical wisdom. It's a bit like having to walk around a town in order to actually know the place.

A list that might help

We can rarely change the systems or the people who cause us trauma, but there are some things that I have seen that are really helpful and form a good grid to work with. This list comes from working over the years with my own students and in my own life, as well as having studied widely on trauma and its effects on us.

Understand that this is part of your journey

But it is not all that you are. Your current situation may be rooted in and expressive of trauma, but awareness, love, honesty and soulful action will begin to lead you in new ways.

Make a commitment to yourself to always come back to love, it really is all we have.

Learn to stop living in the house of stories

Instead of remaining connected to your trauma, allow space for your soul identity to shine through where it can. The clearer we allow ourselves to see from the centre, the better.

Seek help and allow help if it is available

By help, I mean help to integrate, understand, and discover and be reminded of your wholeness again, rather than creating too much of a psychological file that is part of the house of somebodiness. Psychological profiling does have real uses, but we find that healing and wholeness lie in a deeper place than much of what can be done in that field – unless the professional we are working with has developed real presence and awareness within themselves. Then we are most fortunate indeed.

Commit to your healing and novel self-care path

Give your word to yourself, be realistic as to what you can do and keep it simple, but keep it.

If the trauma is ongoing within a particular situation, leave if you can

If you can leave peacefully, all well and good. If peace won't work allow anger to be your friend who helps you leave, and if you are frozen and can't leave, forgive yourself over and over again. This can easily relate to so many situations such as family situations, war zones and political situations.

Quietly and lovingly build any boundaries and resources that you can to help you

One thing I have seen that is really difficult is where a person is in a locked in situation with an abusive partner or family and they need to leave but can't because they have no money of their own. Yet their lifestyle looks well-to-do. I have seen this with women more than with men, but it can be either way. While this might seem like an odd thing to say in a "spiritual book", it is imperative in the world we live in that we develop good boundaries and have our own resources, and that they really are ours. My mum always used to say: "You must always keep something for yourself, no matter how much you love the other person." Freedom comes from equivalence, boundaries and a sense of your inner self. I wish the world was different, but right now it is not, and building your own resources can really be part of your spiritual journey.

In terms of resources, I would say that a good initial aim is to have the ability to live for a year in a new situation available to you. How you build your resources will be completely individual to you, but we can build a day at a time. For example, the price of a coffee per day soon grows into quite a substantial amount of money. A day, a week, a month, three months and so on. This actually creates space, better boundaries, and oneness as things grow. There is nothing selfish or wrong about this, I know in the Bible and in a myriad of enlightened texts it says "Consider the lilies of the field" – for sure, on the level of so much of life and our souls, yes, but I learned the hard way that my mum was so right about this one. It's terrible isn't it that our parents can often turn out to be right, even when much of what we are dealing with may have come through them generationally? That is a big part of the conundrum.

Allow for the possibilities and actualities to change regardless of any situation

When we are in trauma, our possibilities can seem narrow. As best you can, try to keep novel experiences flowing for you. There are days where it will feel like if you don't make your heart beat it won't work. We literally have to make ourselves choose to breathe some days. Yet regardless of the story or the situation, awareness will build toward change, and the more room you can make for it through your practice and through novel experience, the easier it can take hold.

Embodiment and present awareness are always going to help

The idea of embodiment can seem absolutely counter-intuitive at times. Trauma is often numbing, and we lose the feeling of our senses and body, this is why things like acupuncture, gentle yoga and *qigong* have been found to be particularly helpful with trauma patients and people suffering with PTSD. Dancing as a way to allow emotion to move and be processed really works as well. As does walking, running, being in nature, and doing weights in the gym. These are not ends in themselves, but have benefits within them which all the while allow us a gateway to re-embodiment, and to getting the stagnant aspects of emotion and energy moving again and processing. We can't out-think emotion, though that's often what we try to do. We all live physical lives, we all have our bodies, and so we will have activities available to us that can really support us in this way.

Keep your word to yourself, forgive yourself and return to love over and over again

Saying this again, just to double and triple underline this fundamental teaching.

The way through

Turning toward yourself with real intent and giving yourself your word that you will meet what you have to with love is the great moment of change. When we allow this, the world, our deeper resources and our internal guidance can start getting behind us. You may find a wonderful book that can act as a guide. There are books from yoga teachers, body psychotherapists, inner-child specialists, techniques like TRE (trauma release exercises) and so on, that I am sure would be helpful for you to investigate. The purpose of this book is not to be a guide on how to heal trauma, but I hope that it can be a friend to you and help you see your way a little, and hopefully draw your attention to a thought or heart-click of your own which takes you onward.

New support and healing methodologies are becoming available all the time. For example, trials of microdosing with psychedelics that don't cause any "high" effects are looking to be really helpful in healing trauma, depression, anxiety and schizophrenia, but we are not quite there yet with this.

If meditation is safe for you, the three hearts *shenpa* practice from the previous chapter is the one I'd recommend you work with for as long as you need to. It's a meditation that will always be helpful. There is no rush, no pressure, but there is always turning up for ourselves. There is always forgiveness and there is always the path of love, awareness, embodiment and being.

My heart sees your heart, and you can turn to meet this stuff with love.

Bless you.

SIGNPOST 7

THE ANSWER IN
THE QUESTION

When your awareness of awareness starts to develop, things –
I want to say get easier. That's not true in some ways, and
yet in some ways, it is. Things get easier because we start to
understand that resistance to this moment and attachment to
the conditionality of the story cause so much of our trouble.
They keep us from both healing and awareness, and therefore
we are also kept from awakening, which we might say is the
realization of "what is" within this very moment. We learn
to ease back into being, into soul. We learn that what is
presenting itself as a resistance or a question in our day-to-day
life and relationships is, in essence, the path itself trying to get
our attention. Double underlining as ever, it is not our story
about the realization of the truth but discovering something
new and eternal that is tangible but only recognizable to us
at the level of being. As you go on, you will find that you will
be able to conceptualize your realizations if you need to. You
will also learn the frustration of how hard it is to try to convey
the truth to another person. So all we can do is make our
best effort, but actually our very best effort is simply to say
nothing at all – to keep *arya mouna* and discover its benefits
for a while longer.

Something wonderful comes now. When we meet resistance and feel the urge to turn away or look to bypass things, we find that our attempts to avoid responsibility become painful to us. The truth and necessity of congruence become more powerful, and we find that we cannot easily ignore this feeling and calling. It can feel heartbreaking to slip back to our old tactics and strategies, yet we may still be learning how easy it is to turn toward the heart of awareness. In time, we realize that it is less painful actually to meet the things we need to. We might say that we start to learn that the answer is in the question itself. That the door to freedom is waiting for us within our resistance of the moment. One of the great signifiers here is that your desire for wholeness, authenticity and dignity starts to gain gravity at quite an exponential rate.

We start to see that we have our own inner guidance system or wise elder voice within us. As we meet the ordinary situations of life, work, relationships and so on, our congruence or lack of it acts as a compass for our awareness. You will find that you are much less interested in living through drama and stories as this deepens. These too can start to become painful to be around in others who live in them more. We have been sold drama and struggle as the way of modern life, so as we come out from this, we have to watch out for judgement and practice forgiveness toward ourselves and others every step of the way. We also have to learn about our own remaining stories and drama, and allow awareness to go there. Seeing things in others is the easy part. We know all the answers for others. Dignity and humility rooted in authenticity is indeed most needed in regard to this lifelong lesson.

Blockages

While this is a really wonderful time of discovery, and this phase can easily last a lifetime, there will be pain that we have to turn toward. Thankfully awareness is for all intents and purposes love. We are likely to experience pain at not being able to communicate with our loved ones, to share the journey we are on. There will be pain at seeing the world locked into its dualities and conditioning. There's the tough old pain of having to face some of the things we have done in our lives. We've all hurt people, betrayed ourselves, refused to understand, and wasted life and time, and much more. Please listen and know that not one of us could have got here any quicker; if you could have, you would have. The journey is as long as it is.

Our old friend spiritual ego can crop up too of course, thinking that perhaps we are someway better than others because we meditate, or we are on the spiritual path and identify as such. This one is a gift that keeps on giving, especially when we think we are through it and on the other side. Many spiritual teachers will try to exploit this in order to capitalize on you. If you have anything to do with this type of person, notice how they will tell you that you are 'part of the great swelling of consciousness now taking place' or some variation of this. In cult speak they call this "love bombing", and we are all so susceptible to such things until we grow into ourselves and embody the ordinariness and humility of what sacredness truly is. Whether there is a swell in consciousness or not, is not the point. Whether we've got caught by this likewise is not the point. Somewhere in us we know that there is no automatic admission or elevation of status because we meditate or we've read this book or a thousand others, or because we sit at the feet of some teacher or guru and call them master. In the end, which is here and now, there is your soul, and whether you are living from it or tricking yourself and being performative. Humility and awareness are always our touchstones to bring in to play as soon as we notice we've gone. There is no need for guilt or shame, it's quite the merry-go-round. Awareness becomes aware and we humbly come home, nothing else helps. "Surrender, soothe, forgive."

The way through

Surrender, soothe and forgive again, again, again. There may be periods of what seems like depression now as we start to see more clearly how we have been living, or as the reality of how we live as the human race starts to dawn on us. This is often coupled with a sense of wanting to withdraw. We must be careful not to elevate depression into a spiritual attribute, and we must seek help if we do. It's always better to check. Sometimes though there is a real heavy feeling period around this stage as we are grieving for what we thought life was supposed to be from the old point of view.

If depression or difficulty does come, then understand that this too is a call to love and action and healing, not a call to more war with yourself. As ever we need the utmost love and care and honest reality that we can muster. Wanting to withdraw is very common on the sacred path, you might find that you want to take more time to retreat. You might look to see whether you can change the way you work, or reorganize how you live, how you use your money, to better support you. A period of withdrawal is absolutely natural. In my own case, when the changes started coming, I think the withdrawal period was around about five years. With others I know of, and those who I have studied, there seems to be a span of three to ten years if there is a movement toward awakening taking place and the consciousness is shifting into its congruent mode. But don't take this as scriptural, and please don't see it as something to try and get through, for some this is the work of more than one lifetime.

Turning toward the "what is"

What we realize much more readily now is that we have a choice. Old stuff will continue to play out in us, but we have a better choice between responding and reaction, between awareness and the same old same old. This is a time of great opportunity to meet and learn about ourselves and our resistances. Hence, we find the answer is always in the question.

Allowing your increasing sensitivity and change

The theme of allowing continues and will go with us all the way to the end. You might find that your increasing sensitivity and vulnerability may be taken by the world as weakness, as might your desire to no longer live in and through the situations that you have previously been in. In many ways it is like leaving a cult or a gang. The world often seems like it demands that we live in certain ways that fall to low common denominators, and you will ultimately have to negotiate these things for yourself. You can of course look to models of how others have lived and walked on this path and perhaps find some clues, but keep on being easy, keep on allowing yourself to not know, keep on not grasping after certainties too much.

We can begin to enjoy the not knowing, the changes, and the ups and downs, because the constant in our lives becomes that steadier natural awareness and soul sense. You don't have try to look "spiritual", though you might enjoy having fun with outer things like fashion and lifestyle. I personally found that I started enjoying my time alone a lot more; I call it hanging out with God. It's just *arya mouna* really. I also found that being quite ordinary was something very beautiful and authentic. Many of my students, without any push from me in this direction, also have found the shift to ordinariness to be really lovely, and a great way to temper their comings and goings as they learn about their lives from the inside.

Several more things seem to arise in this time and over the next while, namely: boundaries and making amends.

Boundaries

Boundaries become very important, and we begin to understand that good boundaries are a vital part of love. You may feel that you need to develop better boundaries in your friendships and relationships. Yet here too we must go slow; it is far too easy to throw people away. Try to see the soul within the form of the other person as best you can. Ram Dass used to say: "Try to see everybody as if they are God in drag." We must look after ourselves and be nurturing and know that when it is time for something or someone to leave us, just like when it is time for something or someone new to come, it will just be so, we don't need to force anything. As awareness reveals its spontaneous nature more and more, boundaries become more natural and less reaction based, and we find we can lean into them much more easily.

Making amends

You will find that, like every other person who has ever lived, you have created some serious messes on the way. In the old model we usually spend an inordinate amount of our time pretending that we are perfect and that we've never hurt anyone, and if we somehow did, it was their own fault because (insert false consciousness or *vasana*-based projection, rage and reasoning). As you no longer have to do that anymore, and the incongruity of that way of life actually hurts you, you find that you choose to forego spiritual bypassing and can look instead toward making amends.

Making amends is one of the most important forms of love in action. Here we are talking about it in a few short paragraphs, and yet it is a huge area. All I would ask of you here is that you bring reflection to this vital component. There is so much to learn here about surrender, projection, healing, humility, love and appropriateness. We also find out a great deal about whether our spirituality is performative or something real that we can lean into, or whether our making amends is sincere, or ego based. This is a discrete spiritual practice in itself, which becomes beautifully available to you now that you are steadying in consciousness and awareness.

In Alcoholics Anonymous and other 12-step recovery systems, making a list of the people we have hurt is a vital step. I personally prefer the word atonement to amends, though I have no idea why. I guess it's something to do with love and the necessity of setting things straight.

But whichever word you choose, it is a deeply worthwhile part of the journey, so I extend the invitation to you to meet this when you are ready.

How do we know what atonements to make?

There's a question for us. How about we ask the person who we need to make amends with what they feel, or think would be right? I know that the *Old Testament* was superseded by Jesus's ministry, but it is interesting to look at how we have addressed questions such as this over our timeline. There are some really amazing examples of what we are talking about in the *Book of Exodus*. In chapter 22 it asks, what is the right atonement for someone who has stolen from you? What do you think? What would you consider right? Should the thief be blamed and shamed forever? Should they be cast out or reminded of things for the rest of their lives? What do you think you have to do if you have stolen from or hurt someone, or yourself? Should you be forever guilty and full of shame?

Of course, we should say sorry and that should be real and authentic, but while saying sorry is a good beginning, it is not usually enough in terms of atonement or creating a better footing. *Exodus*'s answer is that the person should pay back double the full value, and then they are to be forgiven and nothing more should be said about it again. Imagine if we did this financially, emotionally and so on. Imagine if countries that had built their wealth by empire, slavery and colonialism could admit their pasts and seek reconciliation, instead of keeping up falseness and excuses and systemic injustice. We have to get over ourselves and into our hearts to make such amends. This approach might also be applied in relation to ourselves if we have betrayed ourselves in our lives.

I'm sure that we can find many other examples in teachings from every other faith, and they may be useful maps. Yet however we come at things, or however the person or country responds or reacts, these questions really ask us whether we are open, present, listening and have the heart. When we accept the necessity of atonement, we find that it is a wonderful practice that actually is only painful to us if we are still invested in conditioned reality and our somebodiness.

The practice of making amends can hold so many amazing twists and turns such as: the other person may simply forgive you because you had the guts to turn up and be a mensch; this happens a lot. Or that despite how present, loving, and aware you now are, the other person simply never forgives you and there is no way back or forward in the way that we thought. There are some things that get broken and stay broken, no matter what we might wish. This is a tough one to be sure, but if we meet this heartfully we may begin to discover the true meaning of grace. All we can do in such instances is to deepen back into naturalness, allow ourselves to be further stripped of falseness, and become cleaner and more grounded in being and in life itself. I know, ouch. "Surrender, soothe, forgive." It's not easy. Atonement and making amends are such amazing doors to our humanity. They are sorely needed on our planet right now.

Becoming accountable

Something else that we sorely need for ourselves and our planet is that we become accountable to life, that we become open to understand in a way that is much deeper than intellect alone. We are part of nature, part of life, and through honouring your soul you learn what you have to do at this time. This of course continues to grow and change throughout your life, but the clarity of this time and "the curriculum of your own life" starts to become quite clear to you as it arises day by day. The path of love and humanity is becoming self-evident to you, and you see now that the answer is always in the question.

SIGNPOST 8

RETURNING TO INNOCENCE

As you work with presence, healing, making amends, meeting your practice, discovering more of who you are at the level of life and in relation to the world, you see for yourself more of what is true and how conditioning and projection work. Yet, more importantly, you can feel that there is a sense of something in you that is both original, eternal and new at the same time. When we talk about the soul, this is what we are pointing toward. In Sanskrit, this is called *atman* or *atma*. We might say that the awakening journey is *atma nista* – the process of realizing your soul.

Almost everything we have talked about up to this point can be realized from a logical and psychological place. In many ways, it is of no importance that you do this work spiritually. The psychological healing and benefits alone of learning about how we are built and finding that you are the core of awareness in all this will utterly transform your life for the better. There is no pressure to go anywhere or do anything. You may be seeing that you have started on a rational path and are now finding yourself experiencing more of the sacredness and the mystery of life, or perhaps some strange combination of the rational and mystical. You may have come here looking for spiritual answers and found that the work has been more about practical and material things. There is no wrong way or right way as long as you are sincere. Authenticity is the quickest route. But I'd say that to go forward into awakening is much more about the sacred side. It's not about now taking on beliefs and trying to mould yourself into something. I was giving a talk to a church group in the US a little while ago, and I could see that their working method was based on moulding themselves into their belief structure. They were not at fault for all the force they were meeting this with – that's just their lesson in waiting, but everything felt performative and false. Yet they would swear blind that they were fully sincere if you asked them. One of the church leader's anger toward me was like being buffeted by a windstorm, even though she outwardly smiled and blessed with every syllable.

So perhaps sincerity means just being open and authentic, allowing for awareness within ourselves and not chasing the mystical or the sacred, but just seeing what comes. When we drop to the authentic and sacred, we find that they don't have the names we usually give them.

PAUSE FOR REFLECTION

Part 1 – Take a few moments to reflect deeply on the qualities of your experiencing of sacredness and awareness. Where do you feel it? Where are you aware of it? Can your mind grasp it? If your mind can't hold it – how do you know it? It may be more or less clear and may feel like it comes and goes from you, but follow this invitation often, and it will be a beautiful guide for you.

Part 2 – Grab some paper or your journal and some colours and create a drawing of your heart and its contents. Lean into colour and see what it has to show you.

Observable traits

Throughout the thousands of years that we have been investigating the nature of reality in this inner way, a number of traits of how the unfolding realization of *atma* is experienced have been observed. When we talk about awakening or self-realization, what we are really talking about is the movement to be in life, rather than feeling like we are removed from the isness of life by being incarnated into thought forms. You may be having flashes of this awareness now. These can't be clung to, though we will try. It can take a little while for a steadiness to come, but even now we can see a little more of what the truth is.

Things you might experience

You have a greater sense of the line of continuity of your being. A sense that you were life before you were born, you were life when you were young, and that you are life now. That the human being is coalesced around and intermingled with life, and you have a sense of knowing that thread rather than a belief in it. You can feel the life that you are. In Zen they call this "your true face before you were born". This is what Sri Nisargadatta and Ramana Maharshi both called the "I Am". Or *atma*. I personally like the word soul, but I realize that people can get hold of the wrong end of that, just like they can with the words God and love.

You notice that you feel more intimate with life. People seem more beautiful, because you are seeing their greater beauty, which is so much more than their apparent surfaces. When you walk in nature you might see that all the plants, trees, and animals are also this same beautiful expression of life. You most likely feel a greater sense of freedom, not that your outer situations may have necessarily changed.

You may find that you have fewer questions in you now, and that your practice, and being in the ordinariness of everyday life, feels more like home. A place of love, beingness and answers. All without too much drama or thought getting in the way.

When you stand back from these qualities, you might find that you can sum all this up by saying that you are returning to your innocence. Which of course is what we are supposed to do. We are supposed to enter our humanity as a child, lose our innocence along the way, live a period of somebodiness thinking that is who we are, and then at some point individuate before returning to innocence. That process is mostly left out in our schooling, parenting and society. Perhaps we don't even know that the possibility exists. Returning to innocence doesn't mean that you become naïve or childish, far from it. It means that you regain the sense of being in life that you had when young. You regain your deeper spontaneous sense of yourself, your creativity and openness to life. Thought and emotion are not destroyed but become more useful – through the individual journey that can only be your own, innocence regained becomes the basis for wisdom, and we all benefit.

Looking ahead

As with all our discussions so far, let's spend a few minutes looking at what can get in our way here, then we'll look at ways forward, though these offerings should be becoming clearer and better known to you now, so we don't need to say as much. We will then close out this chapter with a wonderful meditation based on a very old Taoist practice that is really helpful in embodying your awareness and in bringing you into the sense of deeper life that you are. We will then discuss the fourth dimension of awareness in the following chapters and look more closely at the awakening and enlightening experiences and what the truth of those might be, rather than the miasma of half thoughts and beliefs that often surround them. More importantly, we will look at how you can meet and be with insight, awareness, awakening and enlightenment and take best care through these shifts and beyond. We are going to stay practical and grounded because in the end we are not dealing with something out there and strange, we are dealing with the ordinariness of what is.

Blockages

Let's go onward with a look at some things that we might encounter at this point, or in fact that we might experience anywhere along the line. There will be less to say about "blockages" as we go on, not because they no longer exist, but because this part of the journey of awakening is about hearing the voice of your own soul more and making your way with your inner guidance. Let's lightly touch on a few things that might be less apparent still.

Fear of our own innocence

You may find that because innocence is not really valued as part of our culture, and because we have such a strong belief system as to what is normal in order for our lives to have meaning, that any hint of innocence is often portrayed as weakness or loss. But actually, real innocence often is the key for meaningful change and greater simplicity. It teaches us the need for authenticity and transparency. The part of our mind that holds to the old fixed image of "who we are", and that tries to keep things stable around our projections, will often throw up fears of loss of identity and reputation. This tendency often continues for a long time, and can even surface if we have had an awakening.

Should I go and find my guru now?

This one rises up quite often at this point too, though of course this can happen at any point along the way. We feel now that the only way forward is to find our guru and throw ourselves at their feet. We most likely have read spiritual books by people describing their gurus, or watched online videos, and come to take on the idea that we need someone to mediate our way for us or save us. All I can say is that if you feel this urge, go and see. Go and see but stay honest and listen to your soul.

Back in my early days, I searched all over for someone to save me. I sat in halls with thousands of people weeping and prostrating themselves and issuing shouts of love and endless devotion to their "master". I have sat there and tried to have those feelings and not felt a thing. I've looked straight in the eyes of "mega gurus" as they've hugged me and instead of having *bhav* – spiritual feelings – I've found myself feeling nothing except the wish that they had better showering habits. I've found myself tempted to see what would happen if I started dancing a waltz with them. But then I've also sat with "ordinary" women and men and felt innocence and the greatest presence and love that is beyond imagination but can only be known by the heart.

The way through

And so, the great mantra perhaps from here on out, and for wherever you are at is SEE FOR YOURSELF. Lean into the awareness that you are. Test it, listen to your soul, test it and always keep something for yourself.

When it comes to fearing our own innocence, we must not just test the bounds of what we have been told and programmed with as being the truth, we must question our own feelings and thoughts from our very core. Awareness will teach you how to do this. No change, movement or realization happens without this inward movement. Movement is not the right word as it is more of a letting go of movement, but letting go isn't right either.

Much of the tension we feel is life training us. We are being trained to understand that the other side of two is, as we said before, wholeness, that there is no incongruence. Reading it here, or somewhere else, we may think that believing will lead to knowing, but we need to lean into wisdom which is rooted in realization and embodiment.

If the genuine need or feeling for a teacher arises then, as we discussed, see for yourself, but always look from the deepest awareness you are capable of. It's important to let go of thinking we must find a perfect being with no human flaw. Your life and everything and this moment are always the perfect teachers for you. You might have got the impression that I'm anti guru. I have someone I considered my teacher, actually; even though he is long dead I would still refer to him as such. Was he flawless? No. I wasn't looking for a teacher either, but his love and truthfulness were completely tangible. Now I have "students" of my own. My publisher has asked me to write this book for you, am I your teacher? No. Your soul is your teacher. But my students have taught me that some of them need this kind of relationship for a while, so it's okay, but for both our sakes and wellbeing I have boundaries like you would not believe. Two of the main things I learned from my teacher was to always give people back to themselves and to always remain a student of your own soul. I hope you can recognize this here, because my teacher is right with these things. It is easy to see what happens when a teacher loses sight of these basics.

Even more important is the remembrance to give yourself back to yourself. Finding a teacher means that you might need to walk alongside this other person for a while so that you can benefit from the presence that radiates from their commitment to their own practice. Always remember that they are human and are as perfectly imperfect as you or anyone else. In the long run it's not enlightenment or awakening that is important, it's love and freedom. Steer toward love as sincerely as possible and you won't go wrong.

Meditation – simply being

This meditation is one I use in my classes and on retreats. In many ways, it is a development based on two practices which

I've found to be extremely grounding and safe for anyone to use, regardless where they are at. It is a beautiful vehicle for moving forward into present awareness and awakening and is a profoundly simple practice that moves through three stages. I call it "simply being" as that is where you end up by practising it. Each of the three stages can furthermore be used as whole meditations in themselves should you feel like working with any one part of it. This practice is a lifetime practice; there is no point along the way from absolute beginner to infinity where it will not be helpful.

Before sitting I'd like to introduce you to the three stages very briefly so you can see where this meditation is coming from.

First, we begin by simply setting up for meditation and allowing an aware relaxed state.

Second, we then perform a number of rounds of what is known as "the microcosmic orbit". This meditation is several thousand years old from Taoist China. It parallels the Indian Aryuvedic or yoga chakra system in many ways and is perhaps just as old. It is a body-based practice which will quickly bring you into present awareness and feeling the life in your body quite directly. It is a great healing practice which physically triggers connection and healing at very deep energetic levels. In some ways, you can see the microcosmic orbit as being the origin of the meridian system in Chinese traditional medicine – acupuncture comes from this, as do the practices of *qigong*, Wing Chun *gongfu* and Chinese medicine itself.

It is thought by some that this was the meditation that the famous Buddhist monk Bodhidharma met when he travelled from India to China in the fifth or sixth century. His journey is a fascinating one. Thought to have been born in ancient Iran, he travelled north to spread the teachings of Buddhism when he came across Taoism. By combining Taoism with elements from his own faith, he discovered a simple way to directly realize the true nature of being.

A verse attributed to Bodhidharma goes:

A special transmission outside the scriptures
Not founded upon words and letters.
By pointing directly to mind
It lets one see true nature and attain Buddhahood.

Bodhidharma went on to found what is known as the Chan lineage which later became Zen when the practice moved on to Japan. Bodhidharma is also credited as being the founder of Shaolin *gongfu*, so you see quite a fellow indeed. But here we leave him for now, and in the third stage of your practice you simply drop through the gateway of the sense of life and awareness in you into the state of fullness and being. This then parallels Chan and Soto Zen where the practice is simply to just sit. Here you rest in your true nature. In Zen they say the act of sitting is enlightenment itself.

Got all that? Okay then, off you go.

Guidance in the "simply being" practice

Allow yourself to set up and settle for meditation. This practice is best given 20–30 minutes, but just alter it as you need to. Please don't sit for longer than 40 minutes when you first begin, as you become more experienced, you may from time to time like to sit for an hour or so. How long you sit is not as important as the allowing you bring to the moment itself.

Stage I

As you settle allow your face to be easy and notice how a half smile seems to arise from within you as you relax. Allow the inner smile to light up your eyes, your face, your throat. Allow the smile to reach into your heart, and then to radiate through all your inner organs. If you need a little rudder of focus, notice your natural breath coming and going, how it moves your body, but this is not a breath or mind practice. Just allow the inner smile to light you up from within. Continue like this for a few moments.

Stage 2

Gently allow yourself to notice the sense of energy just below your navel.

Gently allow yourself, without force, to now feel the energy at the crown of your pubis; if you are a woman you might feel this energy in your ovaries.

Gently allow yourself to notice the sense of energy at your perineum.

Relaxing all the while as you notice the orbit of life energy. You can also breathe in and out through each point.

Gently allow yourself to notice the energy at your sacral spine.

Gently allow yourself to notice the energy at the place in your spine directly behind your navel.

Gently allow yourself to notice the energy at the thoracic 11 vertebra, that place in the back just below your heart.

Gently allow yourself to notice the energy at the base of your skull.

Gently allow yourself to notice the energy at the crown of your head.

Gently allow yourself to notice the energy at your third-eye centre.

Gently allow yourself to notice the energy at your throat centre.

Gently allow yourself to notice the energy in your whole solar plexus, before coming back to just below the navel again.

This is one orbit.

Repeat this whole sequence in a relaxed manner at least nine times and let the energy flow at its own speed. You may find that it starts turning faster as you relax until you sense a continuous orbit around you in this flowing motion. You may of course sit with the orbit for longer or make this your whole practice. Notice how you feel in your body. Notice the sense of your mind. Notice the sense of your emotions. Notice your wholeness and the space in which all your life is taking place.

Stage 3

When you have completed your orbits and feel you want to move into the final stage of this practice, allow the orbit to continue on its own if it seems to want to. You can come back to the orbit at any time you feel you would like to, or if you get distracted or disturbed.

From the sense of life in you, from the sense of your being, allow yourself to notice the space in which you are experiencing mind, emotion, senses, breath, everything.

Be aware of the space of the room and the physicality of your being.

And in this stillness, simply rest and be easy.

Simply be – allowing mind, emotion and so on to be witnessed while sensing from the deeper core of awareness in yourself. Not pushing anything away or trying to change or generate a particular experience. Just be.

You are learning how being feels.

Your awareness is aware of itself directly.

Noticing that awareness is taking place before your mind, before your feeling, and yet you sense the oneness of your life.

Sit like this as long as you would like.
Meditating as awareness, simply being.
Being in the here and now.

And when you are ready, gently draw your practice to a close.

PART THREE

RIGHT WHERE YOU ARE

SIGNPOST 9
A DEEPER NORMALITY

In many ways, the following four signposts run concurrently, and just like everything here please understand that what we are sharing is not about following a series of linear steps leading to a destination called enlightenment, but rather simply uncovering the path of deeper meaning within ordinary life, which is what the process of awakening is. Everything we are talking about can happen in almost any order. Obviously, we need a way to hold space around the natural human journey toward awakening, so I'm trying to share with you the best transmission that I can at this point. Perhaps the closest thing to a linear series of certainties is the timeline of awareness, coupled with the necessity of meeting and allowing healing from false consciousness, *vasana* and trauma. As you have seen, the movement toward living with deeper awareness quite naturally entwines with your healing path, though it is also, at the same time, independent of it.

Because you keep on returning to natural awareness, you will have observed that awareness has started to become your deeper normality. As a result, your authenticity and the flavour of your integrity are shining through better. You have begun to move further away from the old tricks of seeing your problems as being somebody else's fault or responsibility to sort out. You are now far more likely, and perhaps even excited, to enter more fully into the curriculum of your own life. You realize that the way you meet your relationships, boundaries, diet, interactions with the world and belief systems is better mediated within the frame of loving awareness. At the same time, you are more aware of the dualities of this world and their push to gain ground. This awareness will increasingly show you the insanity that exists in what we call normal life. You have likely begun to see the basic truth that the systems which pass for normality and endeavour in our world will never lead you home, no matter how sincerely you invest in them.

The fourth dimension of awareness – spontaneous awareness

It is around this time that the fourth aspect of awareness may begin to show itself more clearly. Though for some its arising may not come until after awakening. It is certain though that you will experience flashes of it regardless, and probably already have at particular times in your life.

What is this mysterious fourth level that we've kept you waiting for?

It's that you begin to see the nature of conditioned reality more clearly, and you may even have begun to see where things can lead ahead of time. Sometimes you will be able to see the outcome of a situation or a movement of thought before setting off down its path, or you might find that you sometimes have a greater sense of the chain of conditioning and its factors when you turn your awareness toward an event or a situation. For example, going back to our "argument with someone you love" reflection from earlier. Maybe you see that you are about to have a tough time, you see how you and the other person will act if you allow that *vasana* to incarnate into being. This noticing means that instead you can make a choice to lean into your heart and awareness. You can choose to step out of that line of fire, and therefore take a better and more heart-based approach to what is arising. You find that you can bring in some love and healing ahead of time as you recognize the patterns that usually play out so unconsciously and destructively. This indeed is a beautiful stage. Your relationships begin to flourish and take on greater depth. There is a greater sense of your human potential. You may also find that many relationships that you thought were based in love and mutuality have been built on other factors – such as trying to cover over loneliness, or a need for status or power, or the imagined need for a tribe or a party that agrees with you, and so you can begin to let these things drift away if you need to.

The faculty of fourth dimensional awareness certainly seems to be one of the things that grows stronger with awakening. Before awakening it might be quite vague, or hard to separate from just being a track of learned response and experience. It is important to state that this is not telepathy, nor is it a *siddhi* (the Sanskrit word for a psychic power). It's not the same as your intuition but may appear to be very similar. Rather, it is the edge of understanding the conditional nature of what we have falsely come to think of as reality. An absolute penetration of this kind of insight is often attributed to the person we commonly call the Buddha. If you think of the well-known Buddhist *Heart Sutra*, it begins with the bodhisattva of compassion seeing deeply the nature of the causal chains that lead to all of our suffering and delusion.

From ongoing work on a version of the *Heart Sutra* that I've been looking at for years but have yet to finish:

The bodhisattva of compassion was moving deeply in the course of wisdom which has gone beyond.

He looked at that which we call the world and found that there are but five forms which, in their own being, are essentially empty.

As with the other levels of awareness, please don't try to rush the revelation of this truth. It's not possible to hurry, even if you want to with all your might. Nor does any awareness or awakening we might have make us special or above anybody else. Awareness, awakening and enlightenment are the most natural aspects of your being, which by this work you are simply uncovering. It is as far away from somebodiness as you can get. The wonderful thing is that you have begun to see how things work, and as ever, if grace allows, what we call awakening will light your life at the right time. When the day comes that we give up trying to awaken as part of a somebody scheme, then you find out who you really are.

Blockages

Once we have the choice of presence and awareness in our lives, we will start catching ourselves a lot of the time before we slide into old patterns. We might think now that we're done and dusted and that things have a guaranteed outcome. We've said this so many times already, but it's true, ego can get hold of anything, especially around healing and spirituality.

We might be tempted to rest on our laurels now or try to show others how good or different we are from how we used to be.

The traps of various cultural elements can also really be a bit sticky for us. This period is quite a vulnerable time between shifting from the old identity to the more authentic aspect of your being, so a loving and kind approach is always the default we need. Culture is never impartial or unbiased. We may try to adopt a more spiritual culture and get drawn into circles of influence that are seeking to capitalize on our energy and search for truth. In the early decades of the 21st century we've seen people who looked like they were solidly moving forward with awareness get really caught and radicalized away from actual freedom and love for the sake of an identity and the one-sided aspect of duality that we spoke about earlier. Because everything is seen as being up for grabs at this time, many of the places where we tend to look for information and deeper truths have become places of great duality and manipulation, so we must always measure everything against our soul.

Our unhealed unconsciousness, our *vasana*, often leads us to feeling that we need to find a place with people who share our beliefs – this can be a terrible trap. All cults have used this snare over the centuries and sadly we are no more sophisticated today, though we might think we are because we have certain technologies. We tend to think we know everything because of the internet. Everyone can be a spiritual teacher now, but few seem to be doing the work. The *vasana* of narcissism has got hold of so many of us at this time. The talk is easy, but we are here to walk the walk.

There are so many traps, beliefs, and unconsciousnesses that can get in our way. But awareness will in time allow you to directly see how every one of these paths plays the duality game of trying to push and pull you into thinking there is a side to be on, rather than promoting the most important understanding we need right now, that consciousness and proactivity are the way forward. As Michelangelo Buonarroti said:

> The greater danger for most of us lies not in setting our aim too high and falling short; but in setting our aim too low and achieving our mark.

Some of the dualities that currently hold us back from our true human potential and expression include:

Nationalism
Which affects so many countries at this time.

A country's ideas of its exceptionalism
Again, so there are so many countries falling under this delusion.

Finances
Our relationships to money and inheritance, particularly how we confuse them with a human's right to exist within our social systems.

Normative culture

The things that silently pass for cultural norms are from the awakening point of view often really dangerous and insidious. We see from our deepening awareness that they are usually based on the reinforcement of false consciousness. National and tribal *vasana* is put forward as if it were truth, controlling and consuming so much of our daily lives. If you dare to think or feel outside of these boxes, you soon find out the dangerous nature of normality.

Looking for shortcuts to enlightenment

There are healing modalities such as microdosing that are looking very promising at the moment in regard to helping heal trauma, depression and other illnesses. There is some real hope finally coming around changing trapped behaviours and addictions and so on. But we have a long way to go with that, and they still need to be balanced out with all of our kindness and supportive guidance while processing in the world. It might be really interesting to look at this more, perhaps in a future book. Yet, when it comes to awakening and enlightenment, many have turned to and still look toward trying to find external shortcuts such as through recreational drugs. While the chemical path may give us flashes of insight, it is important to observe that if we need to keep taking a thing or doing something to try to maintain a state of being, then that is not true awakening. Undoubtedly for some it is a helpful look through the window, but that is all that it is. The wholeness of reality itself unfolding continuously through your unique being is a different matter altogether.

Magical thinking

We can also still get stuck in having magical beliefs, for example, that we can attract things, or engage in special ways of speaking or thinking that will save us, instead of having to face ourselves and "doing the work". Depending on where you are coming from, this book might even sound like it is talking about this type of spiritual identity and all that other stuff, but it is not. We are trying to look at how we can leave behind all those self-made cages and actually be free and based in the body of reality, rather than adding any extra identity of belief system.

The way through

Know that there is no rush. Remembering that awareness is love, so we kindly turn our attention with integrity to keeping on with questing and questioning what is vital and real within ourselves.

- Can you see from awareness where thought is actually coming from?
- Can you see how the action of thought moves to volition in us?
- Can you see how mind and emotion arise?
- How is your body and outer life produced by the life within you?
- Where does that life actually reside in this moment?
- What is blocking your congruence with the underlying ground of being in body, energy and mind?

These questions are not things to pressure ourselves with, they are to be lovingly explored every time we slide into duality. We learn to see from our inner process how duality is the creator of basic ignorance in ourselves and in the world. We must keep our soul in view for it is the North Star for each of us in the process of becoming congruent.

Walt Whitman writes about this in the prelude to *Leaves of Grass* from 1855:

This is what you shall do; Love the earth and sun and the animals, despise riches, give alms to every one that asks, stand up for the stupid and crazy, devote your income and labor to others, hate tyrants, argue not concerning God, have patience and indulgence toward the people, take off your hat to nothing known or unknown or to any man or number of men, go freely with powerful uneducated persons and with the young and with the mothers of families, read these leaves in the open air every season of every year of your life, re-examine all you have been told at school or church or in any book, dismiss whatever insults your own soul, and your very flesh shall be a great poem and have the richest fluency not only in its words but in the silent lines of its lips and face and between the lashes of your eyes and in every motion and joint of your body.

Always remember that both sides of any duality are actually working for the same end of keeping the existing system in play, whether they know it or not. One aspect of it might look like the bad cop, the other the good cop, or one may look like a dictator and the other the moderate. But more often than not their goal is to stop you from being free and awakening. They seek to continue the insanity in order to profit from your life energy, or at the very least prolong itself through your belief in it.

Least harm
As we live in the relative world of duality, we still have to be able to operate within it, and so as a solution for the time being, I would like to invite you to consider the process of leaning into your true awareness as much as you can at this point of your journey. From here try to discern the relative path through which there is least harm and greatest meaningful benefit. Whether it's your political choices or any other choice, we must be rooted in awareness and the real sense of *atma*, but we do not forget that we are part of the world. Wrongheaded withdrawal from the world only enables unconsciousness to keep on with its division, and therefore suffering continues. My own baseline for how I look at things is that if people die, starve, are deprived of real freedom, or are

seen as less than human because of your beliefs, philosophy and societal systems – even if those things are largely unconscious to you – then you are wrong.

Are we the problem?

Only consciousness and awareness rooted in the true self are the remedy. They will transform our understanding from either side of any duality, if they are real in us. Within the relative world they help us see the more transcendent path that underlies the ebb and flow of conditional existence. We have yet to really choose awareness as a path on our planet. There are lots of things that say they are the answer, or try to look like it, but history shows us that our planetary philosophy so far usually results in people dying, or one group of people lacking freedom and dignity so that a small group may believe they are thriving. This type of duality also tends to feed into thoughts such as "If only we could get rid of all of a certain kind of people", then the world would be alright. If that voice is in our heads, we've been got, and we are the problem. This is a hell of a question to ask of oneself or of one's country or system: Am I the problem? Are we the problem?

There is much that people will seek to debate here, debate of course being one of the main tools we use in the continuance of duality. It helps a little sometimes on a mental level, but real change only comes from active loving awareness and compassion. To paraphrase Baba Neem Karoli: Forget enlightenment – love people, feed them and be kind. Our cultures and countries won't love people and feed them, it seems. If these systems can't find this real kindness in their hearts, who does it fall to?

A personal insight

If you don't mind me sharing a little personal insight with you that I had when I was young – I often noticed that an idea would come to me of a kind of book I'd love to read or a kind of music or poem I needed to hear. Yet when I would look for the book or music that was singing in my soul, I'd often find that no such thing existed. Over the years I have learned to take this as a sign that it means God wants me to write that book, or poem and so on, as the sense of it had come to me for this very reason. This is how I became an author. Fast forward to today with the work I do as a spiritual teacher (oh those words) and it's just the same. I'm endeavouring to share with you the result of lived experience rather than sharing second-hand information from my reading over the years. Our meditations exist because they are helpful rudders to realization, they are not designed to fit the memes and popularities of the day.

I have learned to listen to my soul informing me of these things purely out of necessity. The result is that I have found this way really allowed me to find and live the beauty of my own life. I've also found this to be the best route to really connect with the people who this work can be of real service to. Likewise, they find their way quite naturally to me. Of course, you know my rule of always giving people back to themselves – that too is a huge part of what life has shown me. The point I'm trying to make, is that the same goes for our human actions in the communities we live in, the way we work with people, how we are in the daily world. I'm not telling you this to say "Oh look at me", I want you to look at you. I want to invite you to look to your own soul and find your answers there, because this is where the answers you are seeking really lie. Sometimes we find that the answer is to ask a better question in the first place. As Walt Whitman says, "re-examine all you have been told at school or church or in any book, dismiss whatever insults your own soul".

Hold to the ordinary

We must hold to the understanding that at the deepest level it is our ordinary lives and our relationships that are the path.

Our lives are not really complicated at all. We are here while we are here. We have relationships, we express our life, and we either live in duality and a cage of our own conditioning, or we allow ourselves to embrace awareness as the determining factor in how life will play out for us. We all come here with what we might call our unique karmic inheritance, so each of us has our own work to do, but the destination is always the same.

Now more than ever we need to do the work of healing and reintegrating our energies that have been lost to addictions, systems, identities and *vasana*. We need to learn that the word renunciation does not mean throwing our lives and people away, but rather that true renunciation allows for realization and transcendence, which in turn leads us onto the path of naturally upgrading our lives to be based genuinely in freedom and compassion.

The tension is the teaching

As we learn to attend with loving awareness to the nature of our own pull into the gravity well of duality, and as we allow for the lessons of our particular karmic curriculum to become our inner teacher, we will find that this is the radical and most straightforward path to our awakening. By working this way while choosing the path of least harm and greatest awareness, you transcend the old blockages and unconsciousness more and more. This is far more than any idealistic or moral stance, it is the ground of truth taking weight inside of you. This examination of oneself at the mental, emotional, moral and soul level is one of the greatest gateways to your self-realization.

GRACE

As embodiment in awareness, heart, healing and love become more your everyday experience, you will find there are times when you begin to feel and recognize the touch of our tenth signpost, grace, quite clearly. Grace is very difficult to talk about as we cannot create it, just as we cannot create love. But there is a definite parallel between the opening that occurs on the path of awareness and an increase in your experience of grace.

While grace is not very easily defined, we might say that it has two qualities that we can be somewhat certain of. The first is a sense of closeness and intimacy that does not have the fingerprints of attachment. It does not seek to own or even place a name on things, but it has a satisfying sense of presence and life about it. The second characteristic is a sense of profundity, we might say sacredness. Again, like love, we can know this only when we genuinely feel it. Perhaps grace is one of the deeper aspects of love.

The greatest beautifier

Grace is the ultimate beauty treatment. The beauty industry for women and for men turns over many billions of dollars a year; it's a fearsome domain if you look into its machinations. Yet the greatest beautifier, and changer of lives for all people, is grace. When grace comes, every face and body is lifted by it. Every soul is revealed by it. Every life it touches is increased by it. It is both beyond price and yet it is totally free. If you study the people around you, with your kindness but proper discrimination active, you will see that our faces only go two ways as we grow into the ages of our lives. They either show the adherence to the conditioning – the tensions and the embodied worn grooves of trying to live our beliefs – or they show awareness, grace and courage. However, you might occasionally see some who have been worn down by conditioning meet grace unexpectedly in their lives, often after a tragedy of some kind, and they hardly seem like or look like the same person you used to know. Tragedy is not necessary for change, but often life has no other way than to allow us to meet the pain of resistance so personally. We will often hang on to resistance for our whole lives as its intensity feels so much like reality. "It must just be the way things are" our *vasana* says. But grace finds its way as best it can, often temporarily, sometimes permanently, but knowing what you know, please realize you actually do have a choice. Not by the words you say or by being "spiritual", but by allowing your soul. "Resistance is persistence" they say. It must be true because it rhymes. More so, it's the incarnation we make into the story of that resistance and what it is doing to us that creates our worn set faces, and it is the allowing of soul and grace that gives us the ability to respond, be free and live in beauty, and it's not for sale at any department-store beauty counter.

New glasses

The beings and people of our world will look quite different to your eye and heart depending on your locus of awareness, and whether grace is part of your life or not. We can soften and look for what is real in beauty and grace, rather than reincarnate the conditional and traditional accepted norms over and over again. If you wear these new glasses, life will teach you all you need to see and know. If I were to point to one thing that is a true quality of awakening, I would say that grace is where I would guide you to look. More than awareness even.

PAUSE FOR REFLECTION

If you feel like grabbing your journal and perhaps taking ten minutes or so to reflect on your experience of grace, the things you observe in yourself and others, as we have discussed above, it may help you see the trace of grace's beautiful fingers in your life. You might also like to look at your own way of letting go of resistance to the present moment, or to emotions as they present themselves to you. Notice the different modes you have in how you tend to operate with them at this point in time. Maybe, don't look forward, thinking I have so far to go. Perhaps try looking back and seeing how far you have come. Then your future sense of a goal can be a light to illuminate your way.

Blockages

When we talk about our karma, we tend to think of this as a negative thing, something we have to overcome. I can't think of any word in English that means the same thing so I'm going to stick with karma, but I hope we can upgrade it from its western 1960s connotations. The thing is we each arrive here to live the life that is ours and it's going to have a tremendous range of experience in it. The societal system we have created tries to set a kind of statistical norm for how a life should unfold and what it should look like. But anything applied from outside is, as you know, conditioning rather than expression of life. We can also add to our own conditioning from within by what we input into ourselves and by how we bind to our *vasana* and so on. This is not a bad thing, no one escapes conditioning, nor do we need to. Life will offer you every chance at awakening, no matter who you are. The only question is if you can, or will, allow your awareness to recognize that.

It can seem like there isn't a clue to be found, and yet once you start opening up, you will see everything is pointing you home. But the thought I'd like to share with you here is that whatever your life is, it basically falls into two aspects. The situational aspect of your life which might mean one person is rich, while another is poor and so on, and the other aspect of life being your spiritual dimension – the soul of your life. No amount of conditioning can damage your soul, no situation can diminish you. Yet, our awareness can be covered over, as we have discussed at great length, and it is important to really understand that all situations can change in a heartbeat.

In our usage of the word karma, then, we will take it to mean the unique conditions of your life situationally, and your soul's journey to awareness along the path of your life. Karma is neither good nor bad, but the situations each of us face can be vastly different, from the family you are born into, to the country you are in. You may be born into a war zone, or biting poverty, you may be subject to oppressive or totalitarian regimes such as those taking hold around the world at this time. You may have great wealth and comfort and opportunity available to you, but none of these things is really who you are – they are just situations. Please understand I'm not trying to diminish the impact of your situation in any way. Even great wealth can be the most terrible limitation, and it's rare that it ever comes with any compassion or consciousness. Always the defining differences in everything are awareness and grace. With awareness you are you. *Atman* – your soul within every situation, regardless of your surroundings or culture. Grace is also available regardless of the who, what, where and when of your circumstances. With awareness, grace, courage and the strength of love, it may be possible to change your situation should you want to. If you allow your soul to speak to you, you might feel or see where you can go with things in a more congruent way. Because it is good to align your situational life with your soul, and that always starts right where you are this moment.

A moment for a little prayer

As I sit here writing this to you, I've stopped to put my hand on my heart. I pray that you find awareness and change in your situation if you need to, and I hold space in my heart for you in prayer that grace is part of your life, or that the space within you opens so that you may enter the landscape of your own life more beautifully.

The way through

When awareness and grace meet our karmic path, things begin to look very different. A sense of gratitude and blessing may prevail regardless of our situation or means. This becomes even more so with your awakening. You will often see people trying to wear a face of grace, but I want to say to you, give up all pretence and allow yourself awareness and grace for real. If when I say this to you, your heart answers "I don't know how to do that", then admit your not knowing with love to yourself. This is always step one, and step one needs to be taken every single day because that honesty is the simplicity of the path that we require for ourselves.

Allowing for the mystery

Perhaps the key to all this is the word that we have used so much here – allowing. In this case allowing for the mystery rather than looking for what we think we should find. Spontaneity is a clear signifier, as is a genuine sense of openness and adventure. When you allow the adventure of your own life within your situations with love and awareness, you will find grace not too far away. The situation may be unimaginable to others, or it may look like perfection, but it is your heart that makes the difference in the balance of things. All your soul wants of you is that you are you, not an incarnation that only sees themselves as little more than their situation. This means that the path of your life is uniquely your own. You are life in form and in spirit, and so life and form are your journey. They are your tools, the only tools you have, to know yourself through grace.

FREEDOM MEANS LETTING GO OF LETTING GO

With the arising of grace, you will find that a real sense of being free begins to grow in your heart and mind regardless of your life situation. I have known people in prison who are freer in their hearts and minds than millionaires who seemingly have everything if you only look at the surfaces and projections. I have also known millionaires who have lost all their money in a matter of days and then have found life and freedom in much more meaningful and soulful ways. It is this truer sense of freedom that signifies your path now. Not your situation, whatever that might be. Your outer situation will likely begin to change and become more congruent within its relative aspects because of the movement toward your inner wholeness. So you find you can start to let go of even the idea of letting go and just be in life more spontaneously.

Blockages

The world says it loves freedom, we are told multiple times a day how lucky we are to live a certain kind of freedom, and yet the systems we have created are so far from the freedom we are talking about it's almost unbelievable. The deification of the ego has become the guiding interpretation of constitutions and societies the world over. Of course, this is duality doing its work as it does when we invest in it with so much of our mind, emotion and life force. As a seeker of sacred freedom, you will have seen this a lot by now, but it is always good to sit and reflect on the lay of the land and the voices that yell their brand of freedom at us. Seeing and hearing this in ourselves is a great work indeed. The "somebody" we have been talking about so much is not free, no matter what they write into law, onto flags, on to T-shirts, into memes. Even the belief that you are a spiritual person is just that, only a belief. If you've built a spiritual identity – again, it is deification and constitutionalizing the ego.

I am sure you have heard the Zen quote "Being nobody, going nowhere". This is so very important to understand at a deeper level. They also say that the journey is to become a person of no mark; in other words, your soul has no status that it holds on to, even though your outer life will be perceived as having one. Even the journey to becoming a person of no mark can be turned into a "somebody" thing if we do not understand its genuine movement to awareness within our hearts. We are not trying to falsely lower ourselves or raise ourselves; we are simply transcending the old status game to be who we are. You will find that there is no one above you and no one beneath you. We cannot force or fake freedom for ourselves or others. Freedom is an easy word to say, but a different matter altogether in reality. We see daily the struggles, impositions, suffering and inequalities that the dualistic idea of freedom brings, yet the deeper freedom as an ideal is written into our DNA and our souls.

PAUSE FOR REFLECTION

What does freedom mean to you?

The way through

Awakening's loving touch is everything that trying to get somewhere is not. Awareness is love. You will know your way by the innate sense of actual freedom and presence unfolding within you regardless of the situation you are in.

Facing you

We cannot tame the wind or the sea. Cannot make them roll or blow our way. Taming ourselves comes first, then we may laugh at them, scream at them.

We cannot tame those we wish to love. Cannot make them roll or blow our way, but we can laugh with them, scream with them, or break them in the taming we try, which should be the fixing of ourselves.

We cannot tame love, or the wind, or the sea, we are not here for long enough. There will always be these things. Our joy comes from being the flash, the spark in the eye of forever. Forever is grown too old to laugh and scream.

Both in Taoism and in Zen, which are inseparably linked, we are told that if we want freedom all we need to do is give up everything and allow what is real. We also find this same teaching in Ramakrishna's teachings on Kali, and in many other places. Yet we find this such a difficult thing to meet. Why? Because we try to make the letting go an egoic thing. It is "us" who must let go of "something". This leads us into a place of divided mind and consciousness and can often produce quite strange behaviours.

What I have found across more than four decades of practice is that this thought of "letting go" or "giving up everything" leads almost everyone to a really basic misunderstanding, because we try to meet it with the mind, and we make it into a thing in which we attempt to undertake a letting go as action that we have to sustain throughout life. We do not need to make any egoic effort to let go or give anything up in the hope we will get somewhere. On the level that we are talking about, it means not incarnating into your mind and *vasana* identities. This does not mean that we push them away or that we try to get rid and stay rid of them once and for all. Rather, we can just let go of the grip into those identities. The perfect time for this is when you meditate. It's not something you have to do all day, because it is not really a doing, but it is good to check in with yourself throughout the day and return to *atma* (your soul) and proactivity in the areas where we get a bit sticky, such as our dealings with other people or being on our own. As awareness reveals itself more truly and clearly within you, and as you learn to rest into *atma*, you begin to understand deeply that this is exactly what the texts of all the great spiritual traditions are talking about. This is what "letting go of letting go" means.

We give up everything and continue our ordinary daily lives, our relationships, our work, our family life. By this non-process each day transcendence takes place. What is not real will drift away from you more, and what is true will be realized as always having been yours. This in many ways was Ramakrishna's teaching of Kali and Shiva. He explains that Kali, who most people think of as the destroyer, with her necklace of severed heads and her sword aloft, is standing on Shiva' s chest, who lies there open and smiling at her. All people fear her as she is the bringer of death, but Shiva has no fear of her because he is a true renunciate. What has he renounced? Everything that is not true, everything that is false in him. He cannot be killed by Kali, and neither can you if your path is one of the true renunciate.

We assume we know what renunciation means; we envision miserable monks, fearsome nuns and crazy ascetic sadhus. Sexless, joyless, stern, unfulfilled people. The truth could not be further from that. It is not the act of egoic rejection of forms and identity. It is an unfolding going beyond layers of false attachment and fear, ever deepening as congruence with your soul and God transforms you at just the right pace. Along the way you come to learn that love in its purest form is the flavour of freedom. This is so different from what we mean by freedom in the world that seeks to keep us away from the "single way of life" where everything that is true is the spiritual path. In Sanskrit this open way of truth is called *sanatana dharma* – the spiritual path as directed by your own particular life guided by *atma*. This leads us to a greater truth where we find that we even have to give up the idea of awakening in order to awaken.

(YOU HAVE ALWAYS BEEN) AWAKENING TO A NEW DAY

To awaken even for a moment, is to go beyond appearance and emptiness.

(Seng-Ts'an, third Zen ancestor)

And so, awakening comes, not because we get the right balance of meditation, service, renunciation, practice, journaling, church group or *sangha*, but because it comes as naturally as the sunrise at dawn, and there is a knowing, not a belief, that is total. I find myself reaching for words like grace and love again as I try to share this with you. You know that the other life is finished with. You are quite literally born anew in the unfolding isness of this moment.

Temporary or permanent

In some ways, it can appear that there can be two types of awakening: temporary awakenings and permanent ones. Seng-Ts'an and so many other teachers tell us that even having a flash of awakening means you will not live the same way again. Once you taste your soul and God in any way, you are marked for life as there is no way to unknow this. You can't unring a bell. But even with this flash of awakening, the relative world in time reasserts its influence, and it feels like you have slipped back. However, the deep memory and body sense of the knowing will ask you to go on. You will likely have experienced this. Temporary awakenings can last microseconds or days, or even months and years. Yet the old ways come back in like a tide taking away a child's sandcastle on the beach. In Japanese Zen Buddhism, *kensho* or *satori* describe this brief glimpse into the true nature of reality or first insight. The closest Sanskrit words I can think of for this are *bhav* and *maha bhav*, which mean spiritual feeling or great spiritual feeling when it is intense. You can have many insight moments and periods like this in your life. These moments are seen as being the first step toward full awakening.

The lasting realization or permanent awakening is, of course, when realization deepens. You rest in the truth of what is, and in non-relative terms there is no longer any duality. The truth is beyond any doing or wish.

The movement from temporary to lasting awakening can be a time of deep work, gradual changes and shifts, and strong feelings as the old identity is transcended. There have been instances also where permanent awakening has come to someone in a flash. Of course, we do not see how they lived their life before this time and how it may have led to the great shift in this being. Even then, it is always followed by a time of turbulence, as things take quite some while to settle down as the old life is no more. This can sound like there is gradual awakening, and there is sudden awakening. However, they are both the same – awakening is followed by a much more extended period than you might think, in which the new consciousness learns how to be in this world. Because if you are still here – there is a reason and a purpose for that.

The time between

The time between initial awakening and the permanent shift can be a most difficult time, as the ego, for want of a better word, will fear its death and will bring much for you to face and to heal. This is not really the case on the deepest level, but you can't tell an ego that. You do not die, however. In awakening you are unmade and become congruent. Life is seen more and more for what it really is, and you come to know, you no longer have to merely believe – you just know, and most profoundly and beautifully you realize that you have always known. That you have never been outside of love. You have never been separate from what is.

Some stories of awakening

Awakening is very difficult to talk about as what we are trying to share is beyond both the mind and language, and yet your soul knows its resonance; your awareness and being also knows. Perhaps the best way to have a look at it with you is to share some stories of awakening, and so we will look at some people who you may know and some who you may not. The only goal here is to lean into the variety of the expression of the truth. I would also like to share with you briefly the story of my own change away from the old life. Though in no way do I want to turn this book into my biography, or claim anything, or say "Look at me". However, it does seem important to share this with you.

Myself

2012 was the year my old life ended, even though I'd been practising since I was 13 years old, which was in 1977. I had been having flashes since I was six years old where I would suddenly be in the wholeness of life. I used to refer to these flashes as visions. They were complete but momentary insights – moments of *satori*. The first occurred on a school swimming trip to the local pool. I loved swimming under water, and as I broke the surface I emerged into the light, along with a wave of unparalleled energy – after that nothing looked the same any more. In that moment I knew the sense of deeper being from before this birth, and that I could see the underlying life in all things. From that day that sense has never left me, and for a long time I thought everyone could see this way. It took me until well into my twenties to understand that people could not see what they were, or what was right in front of them, because of their conditioning and projections.

I continued to have moments of *bhav* (spiritual feeling) right up to 2012. Because of my karmic inheritance I was always a very soul-led person, but I was also completely lost with severe attachment disorder and codependency – I sought completion always by looking outward. For instance, I believed that the right relationship would be the only thing that could fulfil me.

Though I was lost, the visions continued, urging me onward, and if one looks back to the poetry books I published at that time, particularly *Recital* (2009) and *Full Blood* (2011), and my children's book in 2010, you can see the wisdom of the deeper dimension of being seeping out as I must have been more away from false consciousness and *vasana* when I was immersed in the art of writing. You sometimes see this too in the work of other artists, writers, musicians and composers. Their work is a gateway to the deeper aspect of being, but because ego attaches to it, they often think that it somehow sets them apart from everyone else.

But 2012 came, and the externals that I believed my life to be had become so painful that finally the form of it collapsed. I had attempted suicide three times in the decade preceding this falling down because the pain of living was just too much. Thankfully God was on my side, is on all our sides, and without having any choice in the matter, everything that I'd been living through collapsed. One minute I was standing in the bedroom, the next I was convulsing on the bed howling. A lost child in complete emotional pain, I realized that everything I had tried was a lie and I did not know how to live, I did not know what love was. In that howling storm it was as if a voice spoke to me and told me that Jesus's life was true, Krishna's life was true, Buddha's life was true, Ryokan's life was true. Even some of my beloved poets like Galway Kinnell,

D H Lawrence, Lalla and Kabir all spoke of a greater life. Yet something in me said: "Even if I die today, I will find out for myself. I will try to understand what love really is, and I will follow the leads of Jesus, Krishna, Nisargadatta and so on." Not just believe in them, but find out for myself. There was actually nothing left to lose, nothing. And so even though I had no idea how to move, the journey away from death began to unfold by the smallest increment toward life. I vowed to undertake my healing and used many of the things we have shared here. There was no expectation of any outcome, I only knew that there was nothing else to do.

I cannot describe the days in the desert of tears and anguish, total hopelessness, and falling back, but my soul has always led me on. There is a book by the poet Charles Bukowski titled *What Matters Most Is How Well You Walk Through the Fire*. It is a line of truth, and some days a line from a poem, or a couple of squares of dark chocolate were all I had to live by, but I did the work, knew that healing and loving my own heart were the only options. Then one day, without any indication of a change, some neighbours who I had moaned about miserably in my head for years were having a street party for their young daughter and motioned to me through the window to join them, and I went out and joined them. The next thing I know I'm dancing in the street to 1980s pop music with a plate of food in my hand and I could feel simple ordinary love. I guess this was May 2013.

The next year was remarkable in that I started travelling to Europe to go and stay at a house in a forest as a way of having some deep retreat time. I had started to notice what was taking me away from my soul toward false incarnations and out of deeper awareness. The four dimensions of awareness that we have discussed began to reveal themselves to me and, as the brokenness receded further to be replaced by a happy authentic loving person, my soul kept calling me onward. I was actually happy enough; I was no longer chasing anything. My idea of living the sacred path was just to live each day in authenticity and heart. This period was psychologically and emotionally better than almost anything I could recall from my past life.

One night the following May, I was staying at the house in the woods, and I lay down to sleep. Something had begun to dawn within. I lay awake the whole night and slipped into profound meditation, but that is not the right word for it. I noticed tears were falling and it was as if everything of the old life apart from that sense of my soul was just melting away. At around six in the morning, I was no longer the man I used to be any more. What six-year-old John had known was realized.

In December of 2014, I had just landed in India to join my partner for the winter and a pain started in my side on the six-hour coach ride on the way home from the airport. I had never known such total physical pain. Somehow, we got home and after a few days of no improvement we went to the hospital where I was promptly misdiagnosed and sent home. I knew that I was done for, that the illness was going to kill me. I insisted that we try the hospital again, and somehow found the right doctor. Within an hour I was in the ICU and over the next three days, I was placed on 20-minute watch as things were so precarious. They could not figure out what was going on, but I had a raging infection that was not responding to treatment and they dared not operate as I was so weakened. On the evening of the third day, my wonderful doctor, Dr Trehan, came to see me and my partner who had not left my side. He told us to prepare as I would not last the night and he thought it better that he should tell me directly.

I don't know whether you can imagine being told that your time is up now. I was forced then to face my death. I remember feeling that I had a decision to make, would I spend my last moments in stories or would I be here for real? I leaned into my soul, and let go of all resistance, to be present with life and my beloved partner, Abha. We actually slept and I made it through the night, then in the morning around 9am I knew I was about to go, and I entered meditation to make my journey.

I'm told that I was gone for about five minutes. But in that place, as impossible as it is to tell you about, I felt absolutely and profoundly that I was home. That nothing I had done had ever kept me from being accepted and loved. I knew I was one with God, and yet was not God. The only way to describe it is that it felt like finally being with the friend you have always wanted, so totally alive and loved. I was spoken to then by a voice, I cannot say whether it was male or female. First, I was given a choice, did I want to go back or not? I was done, complete, but I knew Abha would not be alright. I don't mean that she would be broken and have to grieve, I knew that she would not be alright in life after this, I was still needed. When people talk about the light, you think it's going to be a white light, but it is not. Try as I might I find that I have no way to meaningfully relate to you in language what it is really like. Then God spoke clearly again: "Leave your work, and go talk to people." And then I was back in the bed. I had not been resuscitated, I was just back, and the infection had gone down.

Within two days I was discharged, and we had Christmas dinner at a favourite restaurant after a few days in bed at our apartment. I needed major surgery when I got back to the UK, and even now my physical health still needs a lot of balancing in order to "talk to people". This book, I hope you can see, is part of that talking. It's quite interesting getting a direct instruction as to what you are here to do. I don't think you are allowed to ignore it. If you ask Abha about the two Johns, she will tell you that the old lost John is not here any more. I love him, he was a good man and really did his best, but here we are now. Just for fun I have started celebrating 19 December each year as a second birthday. My death was a completion of what started in 2012, and there is so much more that could be said about what comes after, such as not being able to speak easily for about two years after the shift, as the old words in your brain don't match your soul and awareness any more. It takes time for awakening to settle into your form. My teacher used to say that it takes about seven to ten years to arrive properly. We'll talk about that more in the next chapter.

Anandamayi Ma

"At every breath try to be in communion with Him/Her through His/Her Name."

Nirmala Sundari Devi, later known as Anandamayi Ma, was born in 1896. It is said that she was born fully enlightened and so while there is no awakening story, she does talk about a four-stage process she went through at the age of 26. Before this she would have regular kundalini, awakenings or surges which caused great consternation to her family and those around her. Her young husband thought that she might be insane.

She relinquished her regular human life when she was 26, and describes four stages:

1. She transcended the ordinary desires and passions of the world to allow the sacred to be experienced more clearly within herself.
2. By becoming still, she opened her heart awareness so that she could be one with the *hridayam* (heart) and experience *bhav.*
3. Her personal identity melted away into God, but she retained the ability to discern between form and formlessness.
4. She realized full consciousness, relinquishing all duality. She saw the underlying oneness of all that is. Yet she maintained full discernment of how the dualistic world arises and operates.

In India, Anandamayi Ma is often called the most divine flower of all humanity. Though born into a Hindu family, her teachings are not centred in religiosity or belonging to a particular sect. She would travel all over India in her lifetime, simply talking to people and being with them. Wherever she stayed for a while, reforms would take place, such as schools and ashrams being built, the poor being fed, and the general welfare of women, men and animals being improved. Things changed around her naturally, almost as if she simply gave off the perfume of the sacred which naturally brought greater congruence to bear in people's hearts and environments.

Gautama Buddha

Siddhartha Gautama was born around 500 BCE in the area we now call Nepal. His story is very well known indeed. He grew up in a wealthy family that was overly protective of him so that he didn't even know that death existed it seems. One day, while outside his family's compound, he saw a dead body, he saw disease, he saw poverty and conditional living and realized that all he had been raised to think was meaningless in the face of such realities. He decided quite soon after to leave the safety of home and to try to find a solution to the suffering that befalls all people. It's often shrouded over how he lacked the courage then to talk to his wife about his uncertainties and say that he needed leave to go to find the truth. Stories about him often state that he left his wife and young child without saying anything because he felt his nerve would fail him, and the books tend to leave it at that. It is really important to see this aspect of his story though, as history books and his future followers, just like those of all religious leaders, tend to try to show that their person was always perfection itself. Siddhartha's failings both here and during his journey show that he was a human being, as fallible and messy as the rest of us, and knowing this makes for a more hopeful and honest telling because who hasn't hurt or betrayed someone close to them at some point in their life?

Siddhartha became a spiritual seeker for 12 years, trying every meditation technique and taking every initiation and austerity that he could find. It is said that he practised harder than anyone else as he tried to break the door down. Yet all the force of his practice came to nothing when he found himself skeletal and starving and just as lost as anyone despite his experiences. Not one practice or belief had really helped him find the light, the end of suffering. He decided to give up trying and allowed himself some food and milk. He'd become a famous teacher because of his intensity and rigour, but when news of his allowing himself a bath and some food and clothes got out, all his students abandoned him in their disappointment.

At some point later Siddhartha remembered a day from his childhood when he simply felt like he was just himself and within that part of life fully. Remembrance of childhood *satori* perhaps. He went to sit under a tree and, dropping all that he had learned, he vowed that he would sit there until he either died or found the way through beyond the realm of suffering by using what he knew from childhood. In Buddhist texts they externalize his inner process, saying that he was visited by every demon and sexy goddess imaginable who were all out to try to lead him from the truth. Looking at it from what we know now, we can see that he entered presence and faced his false consciousness and *vasana*, and that by remaining in the *hridayam* throughout this night, he transcended the fruits of his *vasana* and so on. It is said that the beautiful dancing girls offered to fulfil all his sexual desires to try to lead him away, and that the devils and demons threw their spears, arrows and fire at him. Yet as Siddhartha remained in the heart, each thing thrown toward him became an offering of flowers and fell to the ground as a gift.

At dawn as the sun rose over the city, the fields and Siddhartha's tree, all that was false had fallen from him and he was enlightened. Looking around him he realized that the profound simplicity of the truth being right here would not be accessible to people, as they live through their beliefs. He decided not to try to teach, but instead spend his days quietly. A handful of his students from his mendicant days had not quite given up on him – on seeing the change in him they begged him to teach them, and so what we call Buddhism began to take form. Though of course he never called it that. He said that anything that genuinely leads to the truth can be considered his teaching.

Ramana Maharshi

Venkataraman Iyer, better known as Ramana Maharshi, was born in 1879 and while in his early teens began to have feelings that some spiritual process was incomplete within himself from his last birth, and so he started practising meditation and going within himself. He would go very deep and often could not recall where he was when he came out from his meditations. Around the age of 15 he began to experience *bhav* and find deeper guidance within the books he was reading. He was being educated at an English-speaking school but loved to read more widely so included books of Indian spirituality beyond the school's curriculum. Through his reading he learned about the sacred hill of Arunachala in the area called Tiruvannamalai and instantly felt drawn to the place.

During his 16th year Venkataraman had what he called a death experience, where he merged with God. While in that deep place he instigated what we would call today a self-enquiry practice. Questions spontaneously arose in him such as: "Who is it who dies?" He awakened instantly, and yet somehow, over the next six weeks, he went to school and lived his ordinary home life, but he felt that nothing was interesting or had meaning for him any more. He felt he should go to Arunachala and knew that his uncle who he lived with would not let him do so. One day, telling a lie to his brother that he had to go back to school for a special class, he ran away and boarded the train to Tiruvannamalai, and two days later arrived at his destination, which he never left again for the rest of his life.

Venkataraman awakening continued to deepen, and the old consciousness fell away further. He made his way to a temple where he collapsed and became insensible. After about six weeks a local holy man found him looking filthy and non-responsive, so he took him out and with the help of a few others cleaned him up as best he could. Over the next while he was transferred to another temple and then another. He was so withdrawn that he did not look after himself in any

215

way at all, and food and water had to be placed in his mouth to try to keep him alive. He remained like this for about three years altogether, and then slowly started to be able to speak again and move about. Though it took another few years for his consciousness to settle into its embodied awakened state. During this time his mother came to see him and begged him to return home, but he would not leave. In time both his mother and his brother moved to live with him and became his disciples.

He moved himself to Arunachala to live at temples there, and during this time, though he was largely silent, people started coming to him to ask questions about the nature of life and reality. An English policeman by the name of Frank Humphreys, who was stationed in the same area, became interested in him and began to go to see him and even wrote about him. Humphreys records that at one point Ramana, as he had become known, had a series of almost epileptic fits, after which he was more able to speak and go about normal life. It seems it took around 17 years for his awakening to fully complete.

Ramana remained near Arunachala for the remainder of his life, and an ashram grew up around him with daily visitors coming to ask him things from the most superficial to the most profound. People considered him a living aspect of God, and his presence drew attention far and wide. His teachings had a profound effect on Carl Jung who made his way to see him, but on arriving at the ashram could not go in. He felt that if he were to sit with Ramana he would lose his outer identity as the great professor that he had worked all his life to build. Along with Anandamayi Ma, and Nisargadatta who we will talk about next, Ramana is considered to be one of the greatest sages of all time.

Nisargadatta
Maruti Shivrampant Kambli, later known as Sri Nisargadatta Maharaj, was born in 1897 in Bombay into a low-income family. His father was a domestic servant who later managed

to do some small-scale farming. Maruti grew up with only a little education and was supposedly quite a rough young man. Though he worked in an office for a short time and managed to get enough money to open a small goods store, mainly selling beedies. Beedies are bad-smelling, cheap handmade cigarettes rolled in leaves rather than paper. Over time he grew a little empire of eight stores selling cigarettes, and after marriage to his wife Sumatibai they took a small flat and started a family. They had three girls and a boy.

In 1933 he met his teacher Sri Siddharameshwar Maharaj, who told him that his life was not as he thought it was, and in order to find out and realize the truth, he need only attend to that which truly felt like "I am" within himself and to disregard everything false. Nisargadatta says: "I simply followed his instruction, which was to focus the mind on pure being, 'I am', and stay in it." Over three years, he attended daily to this simple practice, and quietly and without any seeming wrenching or difficulty, he came to self-realization, after which he simply continued his family life and managing his stores.

In the 1940s, Nisargadatta's wife and one of his daughters died. It is said that his teacher, who had died three years after they first met, came to him in a vision and instructed him to guide people, so he began teaching from the family flat each day, which he did until his own passing in 1981.

We are fortunate to have many direct accounts of Nisargadatta's teachings from people who were there with him for many years as he taught. Many of his core teachings are recorded in the book *I Am That*, which is regarded as a modern spiritual classic. Once he started teaching, he let go of all but one of his stores, as he still felt that he should have something to fall back on, and he carried on smoking himself. He could be very gruff and shouty when asked what he felt were asinine questions just for the sake of intellectual debate. He was only interested in people who genuinely wanted to move on with their path, but he was also very kind. *I Am*

That shows his fierier side, but other teachings show him as being deeply concerned and compassionate for ordinary people's wellbeing and lives. His family continued to live with him, and he would sometimes pause his *satsangs* (spiritual gatherings), which took place on the small upper mezzanine of his apartment, when his young granddaughter would pop her head up through the trap door. Sometimes she would simply join in with the rituals and *bhajans* (sacred chants), and at other times Nisargadatta would leave his students sitting for a while to play with her outside; apparently, she loved to boss him around.

Nisargadatta was not a learned man in the traditional sense that we use that word, but as part of his awakening, he was able to access from the cosmic consciousness knowledge on many subjects from religions to high-end physics. His understanding of the pain of human duality and the necessity to know the self was inexhaustible. He would often explain that it all begins with the question "Who am I?" and you know what happens if you sincerely ask that question.

The range is vast

I hope that these short introductions show you that the range of awakening is as vast as humanity itself, and yet it is the same awakening. There is no "my truth" or "my awakening", it simply is the return to naturalness. We only know about those who have awakened because they allow it to be known. There are many more people who have awakened who do not make themselves known at all. Often they quietly live out simpler lives or just carry on seemingly as before. Their presence is just as valuable as those who teach, for all awareness and awakening change the energy of the world by its very nature. Anything we can say about the path and awakening is only a pointer and is nothing like the thing itself. It always comes back to you, here and now.

Blockages

"Blockages, how can there be blockages at this stage?" You
might ask. There are some things to be really careful of and
there are other questions that are certain to arise for you
because, although awakening is a universal event we still
move within the relative world. It's all very well saying all
form is empty, even when we realize this form is still there in
the way we have collectively shaped it across our history. For
example, we have created a world in which we have to pay to
eat and live in a home on the earth. I find myself wondering
what would have happened to young Ramana Maharshi
or Anandamayi Ma, if they had been born in our times.
Nisargadatta of course would have found his way. Let's look at
some of the questions you are likely to face, and we'll also look
to a couple of sticky points within those questions.

Who am I now? For a time after your shift, it will seem like
there is nothing left of the old identity; in the early days of
the change, it can be disorientating. The systems and dualities
of the world, the way people conduct their lives, politics,
divisions, and relating can all appear to be utter insanity and
so overwhelming. You may find that you are unable to move
in the world as you used to. Confusion can arise if you try
to grasp back into what you have left behind. You may find
yourself unable to be around others at all, or you may find that
you have been abandoned because "you've changed".

There are many stories of people not knowing what was
happening to them as awakening began taking hold, and they've
ended up in dangerous places or even in hospital with people
thinking that they had gone utterly mad. This gives us pause
for two strands of thought. First, how important it is that you
have laid the ground and prepared as best you can, and this is
the work of lifetimes. So I would encourage you to start your
preparations today with where you are at on your path right
now. Second, it is imperative that we have taken care of our
mental and emotional health and so on, for there are even more
people out there who believe they have awakened but who

are actually deeply poorly and entrenched in one side of the duality trap that we talked about earlier. They are bound into an egoic-based identity while convincing themselves they have awakened, and they are of course unable to see where they have got themselves. Many of these poor people end up as teachers or leaders.

The third and perhaps the biggest blockage that can be in play here, and this relates to what we have just discussed in the previous paragraph and elsewhere throughout this book, is that because we have had an awakening we think we are straightened out right across the board. The fact is that unconscious biases of society and tribe can still be strongly in operation in us, and while awakening can feel so total, a true look at others who you know of who have awakened will show you that there can be some really tricky stuff in operation. Awakening doesn't need for us to be perfect to come into effect, it just needs the space. Conversely awakening doesn't make you perfect or complete on the relative level, though it sure as heck can feel like it in the early days and years, and therein lies the trap.

The way through

The most important thing here is to honour and love yourself cleanly enough to always go back to the beginning, back to the basics, even if you seem to be awakened. If you have awakened you will see there is no loss in this simplicity; if you think otherwise – well, what's that about?

With regard to not being aware of what is happening to us when we awaken, which is what happened with Ramana Maharshi, given that you are here reading this book means at least you are interested in laying your groundwork. What I say to my own students is: "Forget enlightenment or awakening, just live this day right and be kind." On the days where that is lived without effort, you are awake. Lose the goal to attain the goal, but look after your body and your psychology, look after your outer life meaningfully each day. We can only do the best we can, and simplicity and integrity in the day that we are living is the best path.

The old advice for when someone started to wake up was to "get to an ashram as quick as you can and give yourself at least three to six months there". These safe spaces don't really exist much any more sadly. Many of the bigger Indian ashrams have become spiritually themed hotel experiences now, but if you look, there are still a few quieter ones that do have their hearts in the right place. Outside of this, you may find that because of where you are on your journey, the right people will appear to assist you. It may of course be necessary to go through this journey on your own. Though even here you will find that you are not really alone. The spirit of those who have come before you live through books, teachings, recordings and the *dharma* (truth) of what is – it is simply singing through every moment and therefore accessible to you. I would say if you can get yourself into nature for a while and away from more daily concerns, then do that as much as you can, but know that this is not forever, it is just for as long as you need the initial space.

There is some really tough stuff for people in this time too, for as much as there will be people drawn to help you, or drawn to your light, there will be those who, because of where they are at, will come to try to destroy the light or suck from it instead of doing their own work. If you end up as a teacher, although as we have seen most do not go down this route, you will find that throughout your public life there are those who are drawn to darkness who will head for you to try to close the light. Your understanding of the natures of codependency, addiction and narcissism will serve you well here so that you can meet those forces meaningfully and with proper kindness that reflects those energies back on themselves. I'm sorry that this is not a nicey nice, *shanti-shanti* kind of book, and that we are looking at the tough stuff so much. Awakening and the whole journey is a place of great vulnerability, and it is better to be clear about what you will face and who you might find on the road, there is no other way through.

The time around awakening is probably best spent in solitude and simplicity, whether that is in a city or in nature. It takes a good long while to settle in, longer than the mind would like. But your mind will get onside with awareness in time. It will in fact become more useful than it used to be, as it is not running the show any more, your soul is. The mind returns to its source in consciousness and it will be there when you need it, clearer and better than before, without its old projections and layers of reactivity. Similarly, your emotions and your full range of humanity are also yours and yet so much better for being illuminated from within.

SIGNPOST 13
LOSING IT

After some time, you will have got used to the shift in
consciousness that we commonly call awakening. Your outer
life will probably be moving to become more reflective of your
inner state of being. For a good while, because of the depth
of your openness to awareness and the sacred, everything will
seem more beautiful to your eyes. You are awake; you are alive;
you are in God. You know rather than believing. You feel
"the peace that passes understanding", and then there is a day
that comes.

It could be days or weeks, months or even years after your
shift, but there is a day when you feel a slight distance from
what is, or perhaps you wake up at night or are in the middle
of a conversation and suddenly realize that it has gone. You
are back to how you used to be. You might find yourself in
the middle of shouting at someone or find that you are lost
in anger and don't know how you got there. Perhaps an old
harmful habit has resurfaced mercilessly. What the heck is
happening? You turn to the internet, to your books and your
teachers. "Surely this can't be! How could I have lost it?"
There is a sense of your awareness and awakening slipping
away, and you can feel it. You have got used to being awake,
and you may have started to earn money from the work you
do around it. You may have a profile and students. "There
aren't supposed to be more problems."

The things we do to try to get back

Perhaps you go full tilt into your meditation or take yourself away travelling or go on retreat. If you dare admit what is happening, you call up a teacher, or you might find yourself sitting alone with it, thinking and worrying how no one must find out that you have been faking it all along or that you are not who you say you are. You are ordinary, lost again, and who can you tell?

I know this is hard to believe, but this is a signpost of awakening.

Blockages

Blockages at this stage may include getting into pretending that you are awake around others and trying to project a certain spiritual image. This of course is showing us what has happened, that some bit of old unfinished ego business has got hold of the story of you being awakened and turned it to its advantage.

One can also really spiral down into shame, or even get into thinking that the whole thing has been a sham. I've seen people become quite anti-everything at this point, reverting to old habits that never served them well, but were just covers for unprocessed emotions. So those types of thoughts and feelings roll around again.

Many will try to chase after enlightenment again, perhaps resorting to drugs, belief systems or ceremonies to try and regain some ground. Some, instead of bringing awareness to what is happening, double down into their persona because they have developed a public face. They continue to say the right things in their talks, videos and books etc, to a more conscious being it is easy to see that their heart and light are not really behind their words and image.

The way through

The way through, if and when this happens with you, of course, is ...

... heartful awareness of even this. Feel the nature of
the sense of loss or what seems to be lost and drop back into
awareness the best you can and you will start to see the nature
of this movement.

Two kinds of awakening?

It is important to remember that there appears to be two
kinds of awakening: temporary and constant. It appears to
be that there are two types, but of course, there is not. We
explored this in the last chapter, but if you are at this stage, it
is important to come back to this with love, awareness
and integrity.

Swinging

One curious phenomenon that happens often is that after
we have "lost it", we go through a period of struggle and
resignation, and then after a while, it starts to feel like things
are coming back. We sigh to ourselves: "Oh my god, thank
you, I thought I'd lost it forever." We are so relieved. Things
seems to be righting themselves again. But after a little while,
it slips again. I call this process swinging. If you attach to the
sense of loss or gain, you will not see what is happening. Even
in the sense of being lost, allow awareness to see the movement
of gain and loss. You will quickly realize that even this sense
of swinging is taking place within the space of awareness.
Therefore, you are not the swinging, you are the deeper
awareness that witnesses the movement, so how can you be
lost? Now realization can take place at this deeper level. It was
your attachment to the state of awakening that put you outside
of the truth, that threw you into the dualistic nature of relative
life again.

This witnessing and the admittance to egoic attachment is
a hugely misunderstood aspect of awakening. It has led many
people to pretend all sorts of harmful things, harmful both

to themselves and to others. If you are true and have genuine integrity, you will see whether your stage of awakening is a temporary one, or you will witness the swinging movement and find that you were never really lost. Either way, there is still a path before you, the path of your own life. Only negative attachment tries to sell the temporary as permanent. If it is not permanent yet, it is not. It is not a problem and is still a beautiful stage of your path and journey. The goal has no goal. We just need love and honesty with ourselves either way, and time and forgiveness as ever.

Always the true signifiers

Negative attachment or being caught in the sense of swinging can go on for many years and lifetimes, but once you start to see it, you can work with it. This is the practice now, as you allow yourself to discover the space of awareness in which even the swinging takes place. This can only be met through a deep remembrance to transcend duality.

You will come to realize that swinging does not mean you have found something and then lost it. As awareness of the greater space is realized, you will find that this is the place in which grace is naturally part of all life. This is the place of divine love and grace, and yet there is still awareness, and you are still a fully human being. You can move in the world as you need to. You will likely find that there is much less to say, if anything at all, but you can if you need to. Within this grace now, within this realization, awakening will take hold when it is ready, and reveal itself as a permanent spiral.

SIGNPOST 14
NOT TWO BUT NOT ONE EITHER

In Sanskrit, the great realization of who you are is sometimes called *brahmajnana*, which means God awareness, or awareness of the absolute. For awakening takes place inside God, and while we are not separate from God in awakening, we are still expressing as a unique aspect of life through our human form. In Zen, they say that we are "not two but not one either". This can present itself as a puzzle or a koan. From the awakened perspective, it is an "aha – this is how it is". If it is helpful for you to know, this was my own direct experience when I passed away in 2014 and returned, and it has continued ever since. If you read testimonials by other people who have had full death experiences and returned, you will find that many of them talk about this "not two but not one" aspect in their own way. You will find though that everyone who tries to speak about this finds it hard to say much about it. It is something truly beyond the limitations of language. If you feel into the life inside you, you will feel that your being knows.

The whole journey to supreme knowledge is called *brahmavidya*, the path of absolute knowing. Wherever you begin – through your current belief system, religion, nihilism, or even following your dreams and intuition – all true seeking is essentially *brahmavidya*. There are so many paths up the mountain, but only one peak. In the end, through the eternal nature of love, we learn that we are "not two but not one either", or to quote the *Tao Te Ching*: "The Tao that can be named is not the eternal Tao." You enter into the mystery but are never really able to explain correctly to another, except through the transmission of your presence, your being, which needs no words. Yet as we use words as part of our human experience, we might decide, like so many others have, to try to impart something somehow for the sake of all life. We try to help end the suffering that we as individuals and as a species create through the fundamental delusion of duality.

Blockages

The old habit of duality is a great blockage. Aside from the Abrahamic faiths and the other religions, modern western spiritual thought tends to run along two distinct lines. First, there are the schools based on secular mindfulness and present-moment awareness. As helpful as these can sometimes be, they are essentially Buddhism rebranded with a relativistic and mentalist-based ethic. One seemingly strange side effect of this line of teaching is that no one ever seems to be allowed enlightenment any more. It is almost as if awakening and the sacred path have been pooh-poohed for the sake of a more psychological set of beliefs rooted in the idea that the mind is essentially who we are, and that enlightenment is some strange new-age fluke.

In some of these schools, there is undoubtedly a feeling of "Well, that was then, but things are very different now". A sense perhaps that we are "not good enough any more" to become enlightened, or that awakening is simply not reality because thought can't get us there. I mention this to you because you may be following a path like this and be discounting your experience or your sense of awakening for the sake of trying to fit a prescribed rational framework. Even after awakening, denial can continue because of our attachment to a particular culture, and so one must kindly check and reflect for oneself.

The second prevalent lineage today is what we might call the Vedantic school, which is one of the spiritual branches leading out of Hinduism. This lineage includes neo-Vedanta, non-duality teachings, the modern takes on yoga and Ayurveda and so on. It is very different from the basic cultural version of Hinduism, though they share the same roots, just as Zen and Buddhism share some of the same backgrounds but are quite different ways of working. Like secular mindfulness and western yoga, many of these expressions have tried to cut away from their roots in the name of modernization, perhaps to fit a more symptomatic and pathology-based functionality. They end up far away from their original spirit of giving people what they need the most. At heart, it is vital if there is to be a move toward consciousness to know and rediscover the deeper truths of all lineages and religions as spiritual practices and allow for their proper function. Because of cultural attachment and identity, there is much denial of their true purpose, and of course, we have the terrible energy of exploiting them for capital and other materialist gains. The fierce stuckness that our world's practices and religions seem to be in can get in the way here of you having a fuller experience if you cling to them.

Strangely, within Vedantic strands, there also tends to be a sense of disgust or disregard for the body. It is a belief that it needs to be got rid of or overcome or is unimportant and seen as a limitation. We can slip into believing that, once we have awakened, we have no more use for our bodies. I honestly don't know if this is an aspect of Christian influence from the Dark Ages that has been conditioned into the Indian subconscious from Britain's 200 years of colonisation in India's recent past. Indeed, practising yoga and Ayurveda was made illegal during those times. They have only survived to this day because of the relentless spirit of some practitioners and teachers and a few more spiritually open westerners like Ramana Maharshi's policeman (*see* Chapter 12).

If we have come through this lineage, we have to watch
out concerning our physical relationship with ourselves.
We can get caught in missing that our bodies are the only
vehicle we have to radiate our light in the world. The truth is
you are going to need your body for what lies ahead. For as
long as your human heart beats, then there is work for you to
do. Reflect on our three hearts meditation practice (*see* Chapter
5), on how one heart leads to the other, and how from this
place of realization we see that the light of the sacred heart
illuminates the emotional and the physical heart. Because of
your soul, your life exists. So, who are you, and what are you
here for?

Forgive me

I've referred to these two strands of practice only because
they are so dominant in the spiritual landscape at the time
of this writing, and I mean neither of them any disrespect;
both are fine paths that will start you on the journey home.
We need to look at where we can get stuck, whatever way
we are following. It is also important to name the limitations
we might be clinging to; please forgive me for going there.
Through my own journey, I have learned that it is valuable
to name the problems we find so that we can have space into
which we can lovingly grow. This is my only intention here –
to create space. It is entirely understandable why these strands
sometimes take the forms that they do. However, if you have
reached this stage, you are most likely here to go beyond just
understanding and are moving on to embrace your awakening
and fullness. We must let go of supporting systems for the
sake of their continuance and cultures, though they may be
beautiful, and instead realize our freedom and autonomy. All
systems are only vehicles, and as lovely as they can be, not one
is the thing itself.

All paths up the same mountain

There are so many paths up the mountain that it would be silly to try to even name them all, but obviously they include the traditional Abrahamic faiths and their gnostic forms, the Taoist schools, Dzogchen, Zen, Dadirri and so many more. Atheism and humanism, too, can also lead one home if sincere. That's the funny thing; it all works. No ego gets out of this one alive, but we do, and that is the great beauty of existence. Everything is moving toward awakening to what is. There is no way around it, even if we squarely believe ourselves to be separate from it all and resist every inch of the way. It is the very nature of existence itself that it knows itself.

The way through

In awakening, you find that the sense of being fully accepted within the beloved sings through you now. You know that you have never been away from this. You have never been away from God. There has never been a time when you were not loved. If any of the old systems are still are clinging to you, listen to your soul inviting you to step onward now. Through kind action, lean into the true meaning of renunciation and letting go. You can even let go of the spiritual cultures you have been part of and still have some attachment to. You understand relative existence, but you live from your soul within it all. In time, you will learn to operate as you need to within the world of forms. In time, you will learn to operate as you need to within the world of forms - we'll talk about this in the next chapter. Through your awakening, you have become one who is "in the world but not of it".

ALWAYS BECOMING

Perhaps the most significant aspect of awakening is its utter sense of ordinariness. There is the *bhav* (spiritual feeling) and the beauty, but awakening is never away from ordinary life. It is implicit. It is perhaps now when things have had time to settle and integrate into your body and consciousness that you start to realize what it means to be fully human. We see that all duality and war, all the clinging to ignorance, all those desires and searches for ourselves outside are a kind of pre-human state. They are all the path to our humanity, but awakening is the entry into our fullness.

You now know "your true face before you were born". You see the base nature of reality, not as knowledge and learning, but experientially and spontaneously. You realize that you are not apart from people or the life around you, though you are still here. You see with a deeper awareness how difficult the path is for each person, and you know that you could have had no other life in the past than the one you have lived. It was the only way.

Thank you

Thank you to the broken road that led me here.
It seems no other road would have got me home.

Voices around you tell you to be spiritual,
talk a sweet certain way, heal quickly
from all things. Find the positive, be present,
But

I need to say thank you to my lost self,
to the fractured homes, the addictions,
the codependence, the bottles,
the drugs, the lust.

I want to thank you – nights
with a knife held in my hand against myself.
So many nights not wanting to be here.

Thank you road.
Thank you lost friends and
thankfully failed relationships.
Imagine if they'd have continued.

Thank you lost.
Only lost can lead to found.
Only the broken can know the liquid meaning
of mercy or show another how to heal.
Only bad love will know the distance to good love.
Only the divided can know the whole.

We don't have to build and live in a house
on Broken Road, instead
we make the journey through the inner war.
Somewhere in the heat of the noise,
there is the silent sacred heart.

Finally you listen, for there is nowhere
else to hang your coat.

You wash your face
Place your hand where your heart is
and say I love you. Thank you.
I know the way home now.

Blockages

There are so many questions that will arise over the coming
years. Do you think you're all done because you've awakened
already? I'm pulling your leg. Of course, in an absolute way,
you know that you are here. Yet as we have discussed, you
can see how the relative world is formed from the illusion of
dualism, and that even though you have largely stepped free
from it, it continues to affect you as you still have form. The
goal is not to get rid of your form but to learn to live your
human life in all its dimensions.

The relative and reactive world is the way of life for most
people to greater and lesser degrees. It is the reactivity itself that
creates this world as it is. Just as the wind increases the tiniest
spark to a forest fire, or constant rain creates a flood – likewise,
duality makes the world as most people know it and adhere to
it. Awakening is rare, though there are stories of it everywhere.
You will most likely have gone beyond loneliness in your
realization, able now to lean into the loving space of God. You
might find yourself looking for others like you; that would
be natural. As you look, you will find many people, groups,
teachers and books saying all the right things, and yet you can
see who is here and who is not. Saying the right things is easy.
Ram Dass in *Be Here Now* talks about the problem of how one
can travel through a whole country of tens of millions of people
and not find another awakened person.

Two types of awakened ones?

The pull of silence and solitude will be strong. It is easy to
become a hermit or to take a job with as little responsibility

and contact with others as possible. The world for a long time will look as if it is insane. Until recently, right up through the line of present-day teachers, the standard spiritual response to all this has so often been to see that everything is ultimately perfect and let it take its course. You still hear this to this day. "Just stay present" and "All is love". But the sacred is not deaf or blind to our plight of conditioned reality. Each of us is the hands of God, and as we look back through the lines of those who have awakened, we see another way. It seems, therefore, that there are two types of awakening – those who awaken for their own liberation and those who awaken for all. The Buddha described these two different types as arhats – those who awaken for themselves – and bodhisattvas – those who awaken for the benefit of all.

Your light is a challenge to situations, laws and people around you

There is another aspect of realization that is not often discussed, but you will encounter it at some point. It might be good as you move through the world to keep your reflections on this to yourself. As you see the fabricated nature of false consciousness and the causal process of conditioned and relative reality, you find that you can understand them and have compassion for them, and the people caught within their webs. Yet you will find that a number of questions are knocking at your door. How can I live in the world now? How can I obey the rules of the human world when I see the unreal nature of duality? You see the meaningless things that so many have died for in so many ways and how we endlessly limit our lives through incongruent laws, twisted money systems, borders, inequities and so on. Someone who is awake is, by their very presence, a challenge to all of that. If you try to talk about these things in the wrong places or even the right places, you can soon find trouble and pitchforks at your door. At the very least, you are likely to be seen as someone who thinks they are better than everyone else. You will find that many people will be drawn to you by your innocence and expression, but you will also find many who will not like you.

The way through

You are not separate from anyone or anything, and thankfully this understanding of truth is central in all real awakenings. You realize that everyone and everything is moving toward realization. You can lean into this and let the inner teacher, the great elder of the life within, of God and your own soul, be your company and your guide.

You are a healthy cell in the body of the world. It may be helpful to think about things in this way. An awakened being is a healthy functioning cell, and so the cells around you are encouraged toward their healing by your very existence. This can cause people to shift, change and grow quite naturally by your very presence, but it can also cause those who identify with their dis-ease to double and triple down and see you as the problem. The story of Jesus demonstrates this quite aptly. We, of course, understand Jesus's message through the gift of his life. We can also see the same with many others who have sought equality and change in our systems.

But the healthy cell analogy may help you see how you can affect the world, if that is part of your calling. All awakenings are of the highest value, and it does seem like there is a difference between arhat and bodhisattva. The Buddhist lineage draws the distinction that the bodhisattva is the greater awakening because they hold back and remain in the world for the sake of all beings. Remember though that all awakening contributes to the greater good, as does every genuine shift in consciousness toward loving awareness. Every step in this direction that a being takes helps to end the war of duality, as well as helping to heal personal and world *vasana* by the amount of its degree.

The law

In terms of being within the conditioned laws and systems of the world, you may decide to go with them, or you may find that your calling is to challenge them vigorously. An awakened person is, in essence, ungovernable, as you are sovereign and autonomous within your being. To the level that you have awakened, you will see that a large amount of what passes for reality is little more than a series of social agreements held in place by narrow belief systems. Though you are awake, these beliefs and currents do affect you as you are here. So the awakened being chooses whether they want to go along with the laws of the land or not.

Within your being, you are free of all of it, but in daily life you can either go against it or just let it be. Regardless, it is a fascinating interface indeed, and your soul is a challenge to all that is dualistic and false without even speaking a word. This is something that you will meet through all of your days. Jesus's ministry is founded on and embodies this challenge: "I do not come in peace but with a sword." Not to kill or oppress, but like Kali to cut away all that is false. Whereas people like Lao Tzu and Ramana Maharshi suggest that we work more within what exists, we bring the light of reality to each situation so that it changes naturally. The ends are the same, however. We have seen many examples of both these approaches across the millennia. Know that your soul will guide you in this area.

The vow of compassion

The call to compassion is not limited to awakened beings. Nisargadatta said: "Compassion is love in action when it meets the suffering of another." Thankfully we see compassion in action every day. Though the self-sustaining action of duality creates its systems to ensure the fires of delusion are kept burning for as long as possible, human beings often find their way to compassion despite the odds. It is one of the great signs that the light of awareness and awakening exists at the heart level and that it is possible for all people. Compassion for self and others is the nature of the path and is the most effective gateway that anyone sincere can follow to lead them home.

When asked what enlightenment felt like, the Buddha didn't say: "It means you have finally conquered and quietened your mind." He said: "The only word that seems to make any sense about it is that it has the quality of compassion in its expression." He also stated that "enlightenment has absolutely nothing to do with the mind and everything to do with the heart". We see the same value expressed again by people like Neem Karoli Baba and Anandamayi Ma. We see it held up, though rarely acted upon, within every religion and tradition. The choice for you now is to learn how to allow its expression in your own life. It will speak to you in your heart. Thought and action can be shaped congruently along lines that are natural to the person you are and the means at your disposal, which are far greater than you can imagine. You still have a person, and one of the great joys of being awake is engaging in life fully through your personhood.

Lila

One often surprising thing that dawns a few years into awakening is that though you have changed completely, some parts of your old self resurface. Many things will have changed or left you completely, but you may still have many of the same tastes you used to have – for example, your preferences in food and music. You may have transcended sexuality, or you may find that even though you are intimate with all life through your beingness, there is still a pull toward sexual expression, and some of your attractions are the same. If there was hurt, trauma or neuroses before, you will find that they still come round to visit you now and then to see how you are doing. Rather than being so all-consuming now, you can greet them like old friends – "Hey, my old sexual pull in this certain direction, how are you? Would you like a cup of tea?"

You may find that if you were artistic, or musical, or enjoyed writing before awakening, you still do. Yet much of the identity is gone from them, which means they can be enjoyed for being part of the dance of life. In Sanskrit, the word *lila* means the sacred play or dance of life. Enjoy your *lila*.

See what a fool I've been

You will also find that many of the things you didn't know how to do before awakening, you still don't know how to do. If you couldn't wire a plug before, play the piano, or fix a car engine, you might still want to take that class one day. There is a lovely true story by a modern Buddhist teacher who tells of what happened when he came back from many years of living in another country as a monk. He had had an awakening, and his teacher said to him that it was time to go back to the US, that his work had to continue in his home town, which I believe was New York City. For the first few months, he walked around the city every day in his orange robes with his mala beads in his hand, looking saintly and greeting people benevolently. Then, like Audrey Hepburn at the beginning of *Breakfast at Tiffany's*, he finds himself looking at his reflection in the big glass window of a department store. He realized at that moment what a fool he was. Imagine walking around New York like this. He didn't know how to work or have a job, he didn't know how to love another person, and he didn't know how to be of service. You might say that this was his real awakening. He went home to his parent's house. Yes, he was living with his parents while being like this. He took off his robes and put on regular clothes, and he says from that day onward his path became about learning how to live an ordinary human life. First, he went back to college, then started work. He met someone and had to learn how to be in a loving relationship with them. They had a child, and he had to understand what it meant to be a father and a husband, how to cook and shop and turn up fully with these other beings.

Nothing special

The story above is important and quite typical for those
who awaken. The path of your ordinary human life is the
extraordinary path. It is awakening into the heart of love itself.
As you live your own life with the four levels of awareness,
it will teach you all you need. There is no need to live in an
ashram or move to India or Thailand. No need to identify
with a religion, a teacher, a school. Though sometimes it is
lovely to enjoy these. There is your life lived in awareness with
love and compassion. The path is nothing special. You are
already on it because you are the path. How could it ever have
been any other way?

When we get right down to it, a lot of being human
mostly involves births, work, marriages and death. We work,
we create, we chop wood and carry water, as Zen says. We
go to the market and do the shopping and pay the bills. The
whole Zen saying is: "Before enlightenment chopping wood
carrying water, after enlightenment chopping wood carrying
water." Your ordinary life is enlightenment itself. The only
difference is you are here now.

The responsibility of the awakened ones

Please know that you do not have to become a spiritual teacher
once you have awakened, or do anything special at all. Most
people who awaken do not go down this route. Ordinary life
affords so many more opportunities than the "teaching path".
The only reason I teach and write is that I was told to do so
directly in the death experience I shared with you earlier. I
have argued with God something shocking about this, as it was
not where I intended to go at all. "I like teaching meditation,"
I say to God, "but this! You can find someone better able to do
this than me." What I'm sharing with you here is that you will
be called to follow the path that is most beneficial for the being
you are, and we must accept and rise to meet this.

The need for elders to bring change

One last thought before we close, it is time for those who are awake, or at least able to access their deeper awareness, to allow themselves to be a greater part of the world. This might be in the political realms; it might be by being on company boards or in greater or lesser positions of influence. If we don't allow ourselves this proactivity, we will continue wishing and hoping that the world will get better by magic. We have discussed the incorruptible and ungovernable nature of those who are awakened, so entry into these worlds would not adversely affect you if you feel called in this way.

Teacher and writer Paul Brunton was one of the first people I'd ever come across who addressed this. He was a student of Ramana Maharshi's and is one of those responsible for bringing news of him and his teachings to the West. Brunton talks about the need for awakened people to be in government, join the military, and find ways to take the lead. Not to pontificate, but to bring awareness into those dualistic realms. How much longer will we wrongly think that not stepping forward is somehow being spiritual? How much longer will we let duality keep stoking the fires that cause suffering? Who better to lead than those who are awake to be in these positions? The invitation is to work with the *lila* of power and leadership by bringing the light of deeper consciousness to bear. Awakening is leadership. It means you have become an elder by your congruence with life, with God. There is no ego in this, but you use the form of your life and person to bring the light of congruence to the world, to help guide us in transcending duality. We are not trying to convert people to new belief systems; you are allowing natural change to come from your heart of awareness and awakening. This world desperately lacks the wisdom of elders and, through conditioning and belief in false consciousness, we have turned to degenerate forms of power in the hope they will save us. There is an inner call to be answered, and your spirit in action is the answer. Our ordinary days, our everyday lives, and our ordinary planet matter. Imagine if we fed people and loved them. How radical would that be?

Always becoming

As you walk your path, live your life, and answer your calling guided by your soul, it becomes clear that there is no such thing as awakening, and then we are done. The entry into your divine ordinariness means that awakening follows awakening. Discovery follows discovery. You are always going beyond duality into the essence of what is. You are always becoming now and new, and there is always more unfolding. The day is always new, you are always new, and love is always new.

GIVING EVERYTHING TO LOVE

And so, we come to the beginning. The eternal beginning and the intimate knowledge of the only thing that really helps us in the long run.

Give everything to love

Give everything to love.
All your doubts and all your desires.
All your fears, and all that you hold on to.
Give your very name and all that you are,
into the arms of love.

There is no thing about you
that love cannot hold.

Love is your action and your voice.
Just as silence holds you,
you give everything to love,
and love gives everything to you.

You are seen and you are known,
nothing of you is unacceptable.

There is no thing about you
that love cannot hold.

Let love open you to yourself.
Let it make you congruent with its force,
its vastness, its specifics,
its now and always nature.

The end is love.
The beginning is love.
The choice in this moment is love.
You know now that it's not even a choice.
There is no thing about you
that love does not already hold.
It is as it is.

Thanks to you

Thank you for allowing me to walk alongside for a little while
on your path. I know I don't know you, but there is love. I
hope that you have found something for your benefit during
your time with these words. Words are never right, but the
soul felt behind our words makes all the difference. Thank you
for the gift of your journey, both now and onward. Thank you
for your dawning light and your awakening.

With love
John

RECOMMENDED READING

Inner-child work
Face to Face with Fear – Krishnanada and Amana Trobe
Healing Your Aloneness – Erika J Chopich and Margaret Paul
Reconciliation – Thich Nhat Hanh
The Family – John Bradshaw

Vasana
Codependent No More – Melody Beattie
Healing into Life and Death – Stephen Levine
Healing of the Self, The Negatives – Paul Brunton
Life After Loss – Bob Deits
Places that Scare You – Pema Chodron
The Essential Jung – Anthony Storr, ed

Trauma and healing
Overcoming Trauma through Yoga – David Emerson and Elizabeth Hopper
The Body Keeps the Score – Bessel van der Kolk
Waking the Tiger – Peter Levine and Ann Frederick
Yogic Management of Common Diseases – Swami Karmananda

Other books by John Siddique

Poetry
The Prize
Northern Soul
Don't Wear It on Your Head
Recital
Full Blood
So

Prose
Four Fathers

Inspiring books of enlightenment
A Goddess Among Us: The Divine Life Of Anandamayi
Be As You Are: The Teachings of Ramana Maharshi – David Godman
Crow with No Mouth – Ikkyu
I Am That – Sri Nisargadatta Maharaj
Illusions – Richard Bach
Jonathan Livingston Seagull – Richard Bach
Jesus the Son of Man – Kahlil Gibran
Knulp – Hermann Hesse
Ma – Swami Mangalananda
Nikhilananda
One Robe, One Bowl – Ryokan
Siddhartha – Hermann Hesse
The Bhagavad Gita
The Bible
The Blissful Life – Robert Powell
The Face of Silence (Sri Ramakrishna) – Swami
The Impersonal Life – Joseph S Benner
The Prophet – Kahlil Gibran
The Ramayana
Tao Te Ching – Lao Tzu
The Upanishads

BIOGRAPHY OF JOHN SIDDIQUE

Sacred teacher and writer John Siddique has dedicated his life to honouring the authentic in our human experience. He is the author of a number of books ranging from poetry and memoir to non-fiction. His meditations and teachings are listened to by millions of people from every walk of life worldwide. *Signposts of the Spiritual Journey* is his eighth book.

The Times of India calls him "Rebellious by nature, pure at heart". *The Spectator* describes him as "A stellar British poet". His teachings and writings have been featured in *Time, The Guardian, Granta*, on CNN and the BBC. *New York Times* correspondent Bina Shah says he is "One of the best poets of our generation". Scottish Poet Laureate Jackie Kay speaks of Siddique's writing as being "A brilliant balancing act".

Siddique is the former British Council writer-in-residence at California State University, Los Angeles. He is an honorary fellow at Leicester University and is a commissioning editor and founding board member of WritersMosaic for The Royal Literary Fund.

You can find out more about John Siddique and his work at: www.authenticliving.life

WATKINS
Sharing Wisdom Since 1893

The story of Watkins began in 1893, when scholar of esotericism John Watkins founded our bookshop, inspired by the lament of his friend and teacher Madame Blavatsky that there was nowhere in London to buy books on mysticism, occultism or metaphysics. That moment marked the birth of Watkins, soon to become the publisher of many of the leading lights of spiritual literature, including Carl Jung, Rudolf Steiner, Alice Bailey and Chögyam Trungpa.

Today, the passion at Watkins Publishing for vigorous questioning is still resolute. Our stimulating and groundbreaking list ranges from ancient traditions and complementary medicine to the latest ideas about personal development, holistic wellbeing and consciousness exploration. We remain at the cutting edge, committed to publishing books that change lives.

DISCOVER MORE AT:
www.watkinspublishing.com

Read our blog   Watch and listen to   Sign up to
our authors in action   our mailing list

We celebrate conscious, passionate, wise and happy living.
Be part of that community by visiting

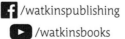 /watkinspublishing   @watkinswisdom
/watkinsbooks   @watkinswisdom